THE
PIRRIE-KYLSANT
MOTORSHIPS
1915–1932

**The story of the 111 motorships built for the R.M.S.P. Group
between 1915 and 1932**

by
ALAN S. MALLETT
and
ANDREW M. B. BELL

©

Published by
Mallett and Bell Publications
3 College Close, Coltishall
Norfolk NR12 7DT
1984

Also by Alan S. Mallett

Idyll of the Kings 1889-1979
(published by World Ship Society, Kendal)

ISBN 0 950 9453 0 7

INTRODUCTION
THE KYLSANT GROUP

Owen Cosby Philipps was appointed Chairman of the Royal Mail Steam Packet Company (R.M.S.P.) in 1903, at the age of 40. Inside 10 years he transformed the line from an outdated concern with a fleet technically years behind its contemporaries to a substantial concern with an up-to-date fleet and investments in several other well-known shipping companies trading not only to South America but also to Africa and the Far East.

During the course of the following 17 years there was further and massive expansion, almost unchecked either by war or the subsequent slump in trade; so much so that in June 1930 Lord Kylsant, as he was now, could report that his companies controlled fleets aggregating 2,650,000 tons gross, with a further 120,000 tons under construction. This fleet carried 1.5 million passengers and 15 million tons of cargo over 20 million miles annually, staffed by 36,000 afloat and 23,000 ashore. The annual tonnage of cargo, by way of comparison, was not far short of 50% of that handled annually at Rotterdam. In addition to his shipowning companies there were substantial investments in shipbuilding, especially Harland & Wolff, steel-making, collieries, hotels and various other activities.

Within 2 years the Group had collapsed under the cumulative burden of its collective debt, and some of the best financial brains in Britain were engaged throughout the thirties in reconstructing the individual companies and salvaging what could be salvaged from the wreckage, resulting in ultimate losses to shareholders of £50 million, a staggering sum for that time.

The purpose of this book is not the financial history of the Group, recently chronicled in considerable detail by Edwin Green and Michael Moss in "A Business of National Importance", but to consider one specific aspect of the Group's shipping operations, the early adoption of the diesel engine and the contribution thereby made to marine engineering, and the benefits now enjoyed by the modern merchant navy.

It is, though, necessary to state that one of the factors which led to the Group's demise was the complicated system of cross investment among the individual companies within the Group which broadly resulted in the immediate needs of any one of the companies being met by other companies within the Group. As there was no holding company as such and no consolidated accounts, it was virtually impossible to ascertain the accumulated indebtedness of the Group. An additional burden was that, in certain instances, notably that of the White Star Line, capital was issued part paid to Group companies. This proved disastrous for that company and embarrassing at best for some of the others. The other principal factor lay in the postwar trading slump, to which was added severe competition on the R.M.S.P.'s own South American services from the Vestey Group's Blue Star Line and from subsidised foreign lines, causing the R.M.S.P. itself to lose money throughout the twenties. Despite this, Lord Kylsant persisted in enlarging his empire and expanding his shipbuilding capacity at Belfast at a high cost. Following the Armistice, 77 war standard vessels were bought from the Government and well over 120 new ships were built up to 1932, many at the high prices ruling from 1918 until about 1922, and financed by loans issued under the Trades Facilities Acts. These loans began falling due for repayment at the end of the 1920's.

It must, therefore, be admitted that the cost of building the motorships recorded in this book constituted a contributory factor in the Group's demise. Ultimately though, they were to prove their value to the nation as well as to their owners. The impact of the 111 ships built may be appreciated if one tries to envisage a shipowner of the standing of C. Y. Tung or Chandris combining with Verolme's to build a fleet of gas turbine or nuclear powered vessels. The first diesel engine went to sea in 1912. It was the foresight and technical expertise of Viscount Pirrie which immediately appreciated the immense potential of this new development and secured for his company the rights to manufacture the Burmeister and Wain engines in Britain, and it was his strong links with Lord Kylsant's companies which provided so many of the early customers under the Red Ensign starting with the first Glen Line ships during World War One. From these pioneers emerged the splendid Union-Castle mail liners of the 1930's, the contemporary Glen Line fast cargo liners, and the immense fleets of today. This is the true significance of the Pirrie-Kylsant motorships.

Cunard White Star

"Georgic"

A. S. Mallett Collection

GEORGIC from a Cunard White Star postcard

4

OWEN COSBY PHILIPPS — LORD KYLSANT

On the face of it, Lord Kylsant sprang of as unlikely stock as any to head one of the world's greatest shipping combines. His connections with the sea were non-existent. His ancestry was traceable with reasonable certainty to Cadifer ap Collwyn, Lord of Dyvett, prior to 1089, and by family tradition 1,000 years earlier through the line of the ancient Princes of Dyfed. During the centuries that followed his ancestors seem to have led relatively blameless lives — one was Lord Justice of South Wales, another went on crusade with Coeur-de-Lion. In 1621 John Philipps, Member of Parliament, was accorded the new rank created by James I — baronet (presumably for the financial consideration dear to that impecunious monarch).

Subsequently the family fortune was reduced, and the twelfth baronet, Sir James Philipps, found it convenient to supplement his income by taking Holy Orders — a supplement that soon proved necessary to raise his family of five daughters and six sons — of whom Owen Cosby was the third.

After attending school in Devon, Owen Philipps was apprenticed to Dent and Company, shipbrokers in Newcastle. Six years later, in 1886, he moved to Glasgow where he embarked upon his first venture into shipowning with the formation of the King Alfred Shipping Company Ltd., owning a small tramp steamer, in 1889.

Owen's savings were insufficient to launch this venture, and it was the support of his elder brother John which made it possible. John had become a leading figure in the financial world of the City of London and was involved closely in the management of several investment trusts. He was also a Member of Parliament and the husband of a very wealthy wife. For the next 30 years his resources were to prove instrumental in Owen's rise to power.

By the turn of the century Owen controlled a fleet of several small tramp ships owned by two companies, as well as the London and Maritime Investment Company Ltd. and the London and Thameshaven Oil Wharves Ltd. In 1902 the brothers moved up-market when John's investment trusts enabled Owen to acquire control of a sizeable proportion of Pacific Steam Navigation Company's capital, and this resulted in a Directorship and Chairmanship of the Royal Mail Steam Packet Company in 1903. An energetic building programme and successful efforts to obtain a new and less restrictive Royal Charter kept his name to the forefront and his own knowledge of shipping world-wide was immeasurably strengthened by his appointment as a Member of the Royal Commission on Shipping Rings in 1906. This proved doubly beneficial, personally because his service, notable for the penetrating nature of his questions and observations, led to his being appointed K.C.M.G. in 1908, and professionally because he had gained valuable knowledge pertaining to the operations of a number of other lines on routes other than the South American and West Indies, some of which lines he was soon to acquire, thanks to his new Charter.

Sir Owen Philipps and Lord Pirrie were well acquainted by now, as the new R.M.S.P. fleet was being built by Harland & Wolff. Each impressed the other, both were impressed by Sir Alfred Jones' management of the Elder Dempster companies in the West African trade. Within a month of Jones' death in December 1909 Pirrie's and Phillips' offer of £500,000 for Sir Alfred's entire shipping and business interests was accepted — 109 ships of 300,000 tons gross. It was not the first company acquired by the Group but it was the first really large concern.

After the War Sir Owen was created Baron Kylsant in 1923, and he continued to expand his shipping interests. Outwardly all seemed well, but one man was not convinced. Basil Sanderson met him shortly after White Star Line was purchased by the Group and recorded his impression of Lord Kylsant as the clouds gathered:

"I found Lord Kylsant an enigma. In the early days of his chairmanship of White Star Line I was not yet a director, but before most board meetings, and sometimes afterwards as well, he was wont to come into my room and lower his thin towering height into an armchair, always leaving two deep bony impressions in its seat, and recount to me the story of his success in the shipping world, culminating with his final triumph in buying the White Star Line, which gave him entry into the North Atlantic trade which he evidently regarded as the cachet to respectability as a shipowner. To have risen to his present heights very obviously Lord Kylsant must at some time have had considerable ability, but I was never able to strike the pitch calculated to evoke the proper chords. For me, it was always a weak and unconvincing treble, with no solid bass notes in the accompaniment. I must have been wrong but when the crash came in 1930 I was in no way surprised. Of one thing I was then, and remain, convinced.

SIR OWEN PHILIPPS

The Hon. Mrs. N. D. Fisher-Hoch

There was no vice in the man, unless it be conceit, and the twelve months' imprisonment to which he was committed was savage, unless it is half proper to affix the sentence according to the damage inflicted, in complete disregard to the motive behind the offence."

Lord Kylsant returned to his home at Coomb, Carmarthenshire, after his release and lived quietly until his death in June 1937.

LOCHGOIL   *World Ship Photo Library*

LOCHEARN   *F. W. Hawks*

LORD PIRRIE

Harland and Wolff

LORD PIRRIE

William James Pirrie was born in May 1847 in Quebec. Two years later his father died and his mother returned with her young children to Belfast, whence they had originally emigrated.

The two major influences upon the young Pirrie were his mother and his paternal grandfather. From the former he inherited the principles of industry, integrity and courtesy that were to stand him in good stead throughout his working life. His grandfather's bequest was an early and lifelong interest in ships and the sea. Captain Pirrie, a Scotsman, had been appointed a member of the Belfast Harbour Commissioners after retiring from the sea and as such had been closely involved in the cutting and opening of the Victoria Channel in 1849 which rendered Belfast accessible to the largest ocean-going ships. The spoil from this channel was used to reclaim a nearby area henceforth known as Queen's Island.

Pirrie left school at 15 and was apprenticed to Harland & Wolff's shipbuilding yard established on Queen's Island. He proved himself a diligent employee and during the next 15 years worked steadily to gain experience in various departments before being appointed a shipyard manager. In 1876 he was made a partner. He was also fortunate inasmuch as both Sir Edward Harland and Gustav Wolff were interested in political and public service and both believed in giving capable youth 'its head'.

By this time Harland & Wolff's had earned themselves an enviable reputation for the quality of their ships and were renowned as the designers and builders of the Bibby Line 'long ships' as well as a number of fine vessels for T. H. Ismay's White Star Line. In the 24 years which remained of the old century Pirrie now set himself the task of travelling the world to study shipping and harbour conditions and to design and sell the ships best suited to serve those routes. One of these visits, in 1892, was to South Africa. The result was a series of orders for 14 ships totalling 100,000 tons gross by 1900, and a connection that lasted until 1959. Another valuable connection was his close friendship with Albert Ballin, head of the Hamburg-America Line, and another important customer of the Belfast shipbuilders. This resulted in the formation of the International Mercantile Marine Company in 1902, which included White Star Line and several other well-known lines. Under a separate arrangement Harland & Wolff, of which Pirrie was now Chairman and Managing Director, acquired 51% of the Hamburg-America Line. Included in the terms of the relevant agreements was a clause that all orders for new vessels and/or heavy repairs to be done at a British yard would be given to Harland & Wolff.

In 1906 Pirrie was elevated to a Barony and in the same year his ceaseless quest for customers brought him into alliance with the new Chairman of the Royal Mail Steam Packet Company, Owen Philipps. The two had become acquainted three years earlier when Pirrie received orders for the first of the new fleet Philipps was planning for his company and the detailed attention Pirrie had given to these new ships clearly impressed the younger man. The partnership crystallised in 1909 after the death of Sir Alfred Jones, who had been much admired by both men. Together they now made an offer for the Elder Dempster Group.

Another important step taken at this time was a complicated arrangement with John Brown's, the Sheffield based steel-making and shipbuilding concern. The stake here was the need to secure supplies of certain castings, flues, and turbines, as well as the supply of armoured plating and other items needed to build warships. The agreement involved a three way share exchange involving Lord Pirrie, Harland & Wolff, and John Browns, and a major factor was Pirrie's ability to win orders in even the most trying circumstances.

The impact of unrestricted submarine warfare commenced in April 1917 caused the Government to create the post of Controller of Merchant Shipping eleven months later, and to name Lord Pirrie as the first incumbent. Pirrie provided the spur needed and in particular espoused the cause of the standard type ships advocated by Col. James Lithgow. In a mere six months he boosted productivity by a real 5.5%.

With the return of peace Lord Pirrie, believing that prosperity and shipbuilding orders went hand in hand, concentrated much effort upon expansion and improvement to his shipyards, which were now working to capacity to turn out the new ships ordered by the Group. The costs of this expansion, estimated at £10 million in 1919 soon increased, and a great deal was financed by loan funds. Lord Pirrie's closing years were clouded by the realisation that, when the postwar building boom was completed in 1923 there were no more orders to follow in his expanded facilities. In the spring of

1924 Lord Pirrie travelled to South America to study the possibilities of Royal Mail opening a seasonal cruising service, and during this visit he caught a chill at Panama aboard EBRO and died in June at the age of 77.

KING ARTHUR *A. Duncan*

PONZANO *World Ship Photo Library*

GLENAPP 1   *Ocean Archives*

LORIGA   *Furness Withy Group P.R. Dept.*

11

HARLAND & WOLFF LTD, BELFAST

A shipbuilding yard was established on Queen's Island, Belfast by a Mr. Hickson in 1853. The first yard manager proved less than satisfactory and in 1854 the position was filled by Mr. Edward Harland. Four years later Mr. Harland bought the business and in 1862 he took Gustav Wolff into partnership.

Mr. Harland was a friend of the Bibby family and obtained orders for three ships from them. These were built to the 'long ship' design pioneered by Mr. Wolff, who was in charge of the drawing office, featuring length ten times beam. The design had a considerable impact and was adopted for the pioneer ships of the new White Star Line established by T. H. Ismay in 1870. This latter order was placed on the advice of Mr. Wolff's uncle, Mr. G. C. Schwalbe, a Liverpool merchant who had assisted Mr. Harland in his purchase of the yard.

In 1885 Harland & Wolff's was registered under the Limited Liability Act as Queen's Island Shipbuilding and Engineering Company Ltd. but three years later the present less cumbersome title was adopted. The founder, by now Sir Edward Harland, died in 1894 and his place as head of the firm was taken by Mr. W. J. Pirrie.

An engine works had been established in 1880 and during the early years of the twentieth century the arrangements with John Browns mentioned in the previous chapter were made, under which Harland & Wolff leased a number of berths at Clydeside for some years. In later years several smaller yards were added to the Group's capacity, of which Cairds, D. & W. Hendersons, and A. & J. Inglis were subsidiaries of Harland and Wolff. Other yards purchased included the Dumbarton yard of A. McMillan and the Ardrossan Dockyard Company.

Harland & Wolff interest in the diesel engine stemmed from Lord Pirrie's visit to Copenhagen to view the Danish cargo ships SELANDIA and FULVIA in 1912. Almost immediately he arranged for the purchase of a one-third interest in the Burmeister and Wain Oil Engine Company and its works at Finniestone, Glasgow. The outstanding portion of the business was added shortly after the outbreak of war in 1914.

The shipbuilding boom of the immediate postwar period encouraged the enlargement and improvement of the Group's shipbuilding capabilities. These were still incomplete when Lord Pirrie died in 1924 and by then orders had greatly diminished. Harland & Wolff was reconstituted as a public company under the Chairmanship of Lord Kylsant and further orders were received from the Group, financed by loans granted under the Trades Facilities Acts, as was indeed part of the yard's modernisation. Other significant orders received during the period covered by this book were those from the Bank Line which totalled 23 diesel powered cargo ships and a number of oil tankers, also diesel engined.

Lord Kylsant relinquished the Chairmanship of Harland & Wolff in 1930 and was succeeded by Sir Frederick Rebbeck, to whom the task fell of nursing the yard through the financial difficulties of the thirties, for the plight of Harland & Wolff was grave. Not until 1944 was the task of re-organisation completed. Sir Frederick served for well over 20 years, by which time Harland & Wolff had completed its 1,500th ship, before being succeeded by his son Dr. Dennis Rebbeck. Now owned by the Government of Northern Ireland, Harland & Wolff has recently received an order for four refrigerated cargo ships from the Blue Star Line.

ULSTER PRINCE   *World Ship Photo Library*

THE DIESEL ENGINE

The name 'Diesel' is derived from Dr. Rudolph Diesel, a French citizen of German descent, born in 1858, who after some years' study, completed a vertical 4 stroke one cylinder engine of 18 horsepower which appeared to work satisfactorily.

The earliest motorships of any significant size were two Russian owned tankers operating on the Caspian Sea, while the first vessel built for open seas was the Dutch VULCANUS of 1910. The real ocean going pioneer was the Danish cargo liner SELANDIA, built by Burmeister and Wain at Copenhagen in 1912 and powered by two of their 1,250 b.h.p. 6 cylinder four cycle engines, to the order of the Danish East Asiatic Company. This vessel and her sistership FULVIA impressed Lord Pirrie enough to induce him to arrange for the manufacture of the Danish company's engines in Great Britain under licence by Harland & Wolff.

Wartime priorities necessarily impeded progress in the adoption and development of the diesel, yet by July 1919 there were 912 motorships in service, of 752,000 tons, while studied applications had included the provision of cruising engines in a German battleship. Ten years later there were 2,933 merchant ships totalling 5.4 million tons gross. In this ten year period the maximum brake horse power capable of being developed per cylinder had increased from 200 to 1,250.

It was tragic that Dr. Diesel did not survive to see his engines achieve their world-wide acceptance. Little more than a year after SELANDIA made her debut, Dr. Diesel was reported missing while crossing the North Sea aboard a railway steamer in September 1913.

The great majority of the engines built by Harland & Wolff in this early period were of the 4 stroke single or double acting designs and the various engines and the ships in which they were fitted are recorded below.

4 Stroke Single Acting Engines

The cylinders of the four stroke single acting Harland & Wolff/Burmeister and Wain engine were supported on A frames, separated by distance pieces, and further reinforced by vertical tie-bolts extending from the top of the cylinder cover to the underside of the bed-plate. The camshaft was level with the cylinder bottoms, and driven from the crank-shaft by a chain drive at the centre of the engine. One fuel pump was used for each cylinder, with airless fuel injection, water-cooled cylinder jackets and oil-cooled pistons. 127 engines of this type were installed in 77 ships built for the Group, as follows:-

Cylinder Dimensions $24\frac{13}{16}'' - 33\frac{1}{2}''$

1. 6 Cylinders		1300 b.h.p.	built 1915-1917
Glenavy	(2)	Glen Line	
Glengyle	(2)	Glen Line	

Cylinder Dimensions $26\frac{3}{8}'' - 39\frac{3}{8}''$

2. 6 Cylinders		1500 b.h.p.	built 1915-1923
Glenade	(2)	Glen Line	
Glenamoy	(2)	Glen Line	
Glenartney	(2)	Glen Line	
Glenluce	(2)	Glen Line	
Glentara	(2)	Glen Line	
Ediba/Mattawin	(2)	Elder Dempster	
Leighton	(2)	Lamport and Holt	
La Paz	(2)	P.S.N.C.	
Lobos	(2)	P.S.N.C.	
Losada	(2)	P.S.N.C.	

Cylinder Dimensions $29\frac{1}{2}'' - 43\frac{1}{16}''$

3. 8 Cylinders		2400 b.h.p.	built 1918
Aba	(2)	Elder Dempster	(completed as Glenapp)

13

Cylinder Dimensions $29\frac{1}{8}'' - 39\frac{3}{8}''$

4. 6 Cylinders   1500 b.h.p.   built 1919

     Glenariffe   (2)   Glen Line

Cylinder Dimensions $29\frac{1}{8}'' - 45\frac{1}{4}''$

5. 8 Cylinders   2500 b.h.p.   built 1920-1924

Glenapp II	(2)	Glen Line
Glenbeg	(2)	Glen Line
Glengarry	(2)	Glen Line
Glenogle	(2)	Glen Line
Glenshiel	(2)	Glen Line
Lochgoil	(2)	R.M.S.P.
Lochkatrine	(2)	R.M.S.P.
Lochmonar	(2)	R.M.S.P.
Adda	(2)	Elder Dempster

Cylinder Dimensions $26\frac{3}{4}'' - 43\frac{5}{16}''$

6. 6 Cylinders   1750 b.h.p.   built 1921-1923

Lassell	(2)	Lamport and Holt
Linnell	(2)	Lamport and Holt
Laguna	(2)	P.S.N.C.

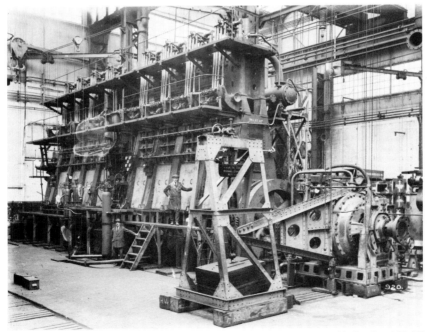

GLENGARRY. Main Engine   *Harland and Wolff*

Cylinder Dimensions $29\frac{1}{8}''-59\frac{1}{16}''$

7. 8 Cylinders		4250 b.h.p.	built 1929-1930
Llangibby Castle	(2)	Union-Castle	
Achimota	(2)	Elder Dempster	
Alfred Jones		Elder Dempster	
David Livingstone		Elder Dempster	
Edward Blyden		Elder Dempster	
Henry Stanley		Elder Dempster	
Macgregor Laird		Elder Dempster	
Mary Slessor		Elder Dempster	
William Wilberforce		Elder Dempster	

8. 6 Cylinders		3100 b.h.p. maximum	built 1925-1930
Dunbar Castle	(2)	Union-Castle	
King Arthur		King Line	(1850 b.h.p.)
King Edgar		King Line	(1850 b.h.p.)
King Edwin		King Line	(1850 b.h.p.)
King Egbert		King Line	(1850 b.h.p.)
King James		British Motorship Co.	(1850 b.h.p.)
King John		King Line	(1850 b.h.p.)
King Lud		King Line	(1850 b.h.p.)
King Malcolm		British Motorship Co.	(1850 b.h.p.)
King Neptune		King Line	(1850 b.h.p.)
King Stephen		King Line	(1850 b.h.p.)
King William		King Line	(1850 b.h.p.)
Araby		MacIver	(1850 b.h.p.)
Gascony		MacIver	(1850 b.h.p.)
Dagomba		Elder Dempster	(1850 b.h.p.)
Daru		Elder Dempster	(1850 b.h.p.)
Deido		Elder Dempster	(1850 b.h.p.)
Dixcove		Elder Dempster	(1850 b.h.p.)
Dunkwa		Elder Dempster	(1850 b.h.p.)

Cylinder Dimensions $15\frac{3}{4}''-29\frac{1}{2}''$

9. 6 Cylinders		590 b.h.p.	built 1925-1931
Amberes	(2)	Mihanovich	
Barcelona	(2)	Mihanovich	
Hamburgo/Atenas	(2)	Mihanovich	
Cardiff	(2)	Mihanovich	
Ciudad de Asuncion	(3)	Mihanovich	
Ciudad de Corrientes	(3)	Mihanovich	
Genova	(2)	Mihanovich	
Glasgow	(2)	Mihanovich	
Madrid	(2)	Mihanovich	
Roma	(2)	Mihanovich	

Cylinder Dimensions $24''-51''$

10. 6 Cylinders	1500 b.h.p.	built 1927-1928
Pacheco	Macandrews	
Palacio	Macandrews	
Pelayo	Macandrews	
Pinto	Macandrews	
Ponzano	Macandrews	

Cylinder Dimensions $29''-72\frac{3}{4}''$

11. 8 Cylinders	2500 b.h.p.	built 1928
Brittany	MacIver	

Cylinder Dimensions 24" — 38"

12. 10 Cylinders   2500 b.h.p.   built 1929-1930

Ulster Monarch	(2)	Belfast S.S. Co.
Ulster Prince	(2)	Belfast S.S. Co.,
Ulster Queen	(2)	Belfast S.S. Co.
Innisfallen	(2)	City of Cork Steam Packet Co.

Cylinder Dimensions 12" — 21"

13. 6 Cylinders   400 b.h.p.   built 1930

Ciudad de Concepcion	(2)	Mihanovich
Guayra	(2)	Mihanovich

Cylinder Dimensions $24\frac{13}{16}$" — $47\frac{1}{4}$"

14. 12 Cylinders   5500 b.h.p.   built 1931

Reina del Pacifico	(4)	P.S.N.C.

REINA DEL PACIFICO. The engine room   *Harland and Wolff*

4 Stroke Double Acting Engines

The Burmeister and Wain 4 stroke double acting engines made their debut aboard the Swedish liner "Gripsholm", and 30 Harland & Wolff built engines of this type were fitted in 15 passenger liners built for the Group between 1925 and 1931.
The engines used were:-

Cylinder Dimensions 33" — 59"

1. 8 Cylinders   6500 b.h.p.   built 1925-1927

Asturias	(2)	R.M.S.P.
Alcantara	(2)	R.M.S.P.
Carnarvon Castle	(2)	Union-Castle

Cylinder Dimensions $26\frac{3}{4}'' - 55\frac{1}{8}''$

2. 8 Cylinders		3250 b.h.p.	built 1926-1927
Accra	(2)	Elder Dempster	
Apapa	(2)	Elder Dempster	

Cylinder Dimensions $26\frac{3}{4}'' - 63''$

3. 8 Cylinders		4750 b.h.p.	built 1928-1932
Highland Brigade	(2)	Nelson	
Highland Chieftain	(2)	Nelson	
Highland Hope	(2)	Nelson	
Highland Monarch	(2)	Nelson	
Highland Patriot	(2)	Nelson	
Highland Princess	(2)	Nelson	

Cylinder Dimensions $33'' - 63''$

4. 10 Cylinders		8500 b.h.p.	built 1930-1932
Britannic	(2)	White Star	
Georgic	(2)	White Star	

5. 8 Cylinders		7000 b.h.p.	built 1930-1931
Warwick Castle	(2)	Union-Castle	
Winchester Castle	(2)	Union-Castle	

CARNARVON CASTLE. Back of the main engines　　　　*Harland and Wolff*

BRITANNIC. One of her engines under construction   *Harland and Wolff*

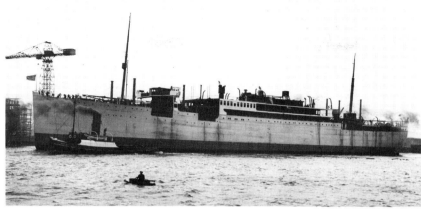

HIGHLAND BRIGADE after launching   *Harland & Wolff*

Engines by other builders

Three vessels were engined with Burmeister and Wain engines built by J. & G. Kincaid of Glasgow. They were all of the 4 stroke single acting type:-

Cylinder Dimensions $24\frac{13}{16}''$ — $51\frac{3}{16}''$

1. 8 Cylinders   1750 b.h.p.   built 1927-1929

    Kheti   Moss Hutchinson
    Kufra   Moss Hutchinson

Cylinder Dimensions $29\frac{1}{8}''$ — $59\frac{1}{16}''$

2. 8 Cylinders   4250 b.h.p.   built 1930

    Mary Kingsley   Elder Dempster

Ships not powered by Burmeister and Wain engines

1. Sulzer 2 stroke single acting 6 Cylinder engines, cylinder dimensions 31'' — 43'', of 2200 b.h.p. powered:-

Coptic	(2)	Shaw Savill & Albion
Karamea	(2)	Shaw Savill & Albion
Taranaki	(2)	Shaw Savill & Albion
Zealandic	(2)	Shaw Savill & Albion

2. Tosi 4 stroke single acting 6 Cylinder engines, cylinder dimensions $24\frac{7}{16}''$ — $38\frac{3}{8}''$, of 1250 b.h.p. powered:-

Pinzon	Macandrews
Pizarro	Macandrews

Ten smaller vessels built for David MacBrayne and for The Argentine Navigation Company were powered by engines variously built by J. & G. Bolinder Ansaldo, Gardners and Metropolitan Vickers. None of these vessels was ocean-going.

ALCANTARA at Buenos Aires

FLEET LISTS PART ONE

Chronology of the 86 Ocean-going Motorships operated by the member and associated companies of the Kylsant Group.

1. Details are extracted from Lloyds Registers.
2. Ships are listed in order of acquisition by their owners. When a ship was owned by more than one Group company full details are recorded under the first owner and reference is made to this under subsequent owners. In all cases the dates following the name are those of entering and leaving the fleet.
3. On the first line is given the ship's official Number (ON) in the British registry followed by her tonnage gross ('g'), nett ('n') and deadweight ('d'), and her dimensions. Deadweight tonnages are approximate. Minor variations in tonnage measurements during a ship's career have been ignored. Dimensions are the registered dimensions — length between perpendiculars x breadth x moulded depth — in feet and tenths of a foot. Where available alternative details given are length overall and loaded draught. All measurements have been expressed in Imperial measures. Engine details given include number and size of cylinders, working particulars and brake horse-power.
4. Only one vessel now remains afloat and her history is believed correct to February 1984.

ROYAL MAIL STEAM PACKET COMPANY

The Royal Mail Steam Packet Company was incorporated by Royal Charter in 1839 to activate proposals drawn up by James MacQueen for the provision of a reliable mail steamship service between Europe and the West Indies. This was intended as the first practical application of MacQueen's detailed 'General Plan for a Mail Communication between Great Britain and the Eastern and Western Ports of the World', which study, interestingly, incorporated evaluation of 'a Central American Canal at no distant date'. For the present, though, the British Government was content to limit the new venture to the West Indies. The capital of the new company was £1.5 million, and 2 steamers were bought and 14 ordered to be built.

The original fleet, and their successors for some 20 years were built under tight control of the Admiralty. This involved wooden hulls, paddle propulsion, and the ability to carry heavy armament at short notice. Only after 1854, when the new AMAZON was burnt out on her maiden voyage, was iron permitted for construction of mailships. Five years later the screw propeller finally supplanted the paddle wheel as prime mover.

It is difficult, in an age of high speed transport and communication, to realise the importance of the new service to the then isolated outposts in the Caribbean. From the start there was little distinction made between territories owing allegiance to Queen Victoria and those under control of less august rulers. A comprehensive fortnightly service speedily evolved, coupled to complex inter-island services with locally based vessels. Despite disruption at the hands of tropical diseases and the occasional hurricane the system worked well, and by the early 1860's the feeder services had been extended to the South American mainland. The logical development of this was the institution of calls by the ocean steamers at Vigo and Lisbon, and in June 1869, the inauguration of a monthly through service from Southampton to Buenos Aires, increased to once a fortnight in 1872.

Despite the wide range of services, a glance at the map is enough to make it clear that it is virtually impossible to provide a service sufficiently comprehensive to enable each of the principal islands to feel that it is getting its service first. In this respect the people of Jamaica were especially dissatisfied and this culminated in 1875 in the formation of the Imperial Direct West Indies Line which immediately secured the contract to carry the Jamaica mails. Over the next 30 years the early services provided by the R.M.S.P. were forgotten as the West Indies operation went into a decline, culminating in 1905 when the newcomers secured the mail contract and fifteen years later when the last R.M.S.P. sailing took place. By now, however, the South American continent had taken first place in the Line's schedules.

The development of the fleet was inhibited by several factors in the 1890's. There were trade problems, and a lack of modern ports which could take the largest liners, and a Court of Directors which was decades behind the times. In 1900 the largest R.M.S.P. liner was the 6,000-ton DANUBE, less than half the size of her Union-Castle contemporaries, also sailing southwards from Southampton. This, coupled with an inability to pay the dividend, finally caused Admiral Chatfield to resign as Chairman and led to the appointment of Owen Philipps as a Director and shortly afterwards Chairman.

The transformation was soon apparent. New cargo ships were rapidly followed by a new class of passenger and mail liner, fully the peer of any in the Merchant Navy. Lord Pirrie saw to that, for the new ships were built at his Belfast yards. A third, less obvious, change was the granting of a new Charter in July 1904, no longer restricting the company to shipowning but empowering it amongst other things to acquire shares in other concerns . . . The new directorate were not slow to make use of these powers.

After the war R.M.S.P. were faced with a particularly difficult trading situation. The Vestey family, with extensive interests in South American meat production, had introduced their own fleet, the Blue Star Line, to carry frozen meat and, from 1927, passengers. French and German rivals were eager to erode the premier mail service and both introduced spectacular new vessels towards the end of the 1920's which eclipsed the Royal Mail liners. An effort to break into the North Atlantic trade proved less than successful.

Only 5 motorships were completed for the parent company of the Group, the first 3 being cargo vessels which proved generally satisfactory in service. The other 2 were the large liners ASTURIAS and ALCANTARA, considered in detail in the chapter on express liners. These 5 apart, no vessels were built for the company between 1920 and 1938. By then, a new company had been formed to take over the fleet of the old, and also to include 2 of the erstwhile subsidiaries on the South American route, Nelson Line and D. & C. MacIver. Money was scarce and only in the late 1930's could new tonnage be contemplated, one diesel engined cargo vessel, LOCHAVON, to become a war casualty, and one new turbine mail steamer, ANDES. This was hardly surprising as in 1934 the motor passenger liners built in the 1920's had been re-engined with steam turbines.

The former Nelson liners maintained the secondary services from 1932 until their replacement in 1959-60 by a new trio of liners, Belfast built and diesel powered. Unfortunately, they only remained on the route for some 8 years before transfer to Shaw Savill, now a fellow member of the Furness Withy Group. All 3 were sold in 1971-2, together with ANDES, and since then Royal Mail Lines has virtually ceased to be a shipowning concern.

FLEET LIST

R1. LOCHKATRINE (1922-1942)

ON. 146228. 9409g. 5812n. 11580d. 485.4 x 62.3 x 35.8/29.6
4SCSA. 16 cyl: $29\frac{1}{8}''-45\frac{1}{4}''$. 5000bhp. 2 screws. 13k.
1.1922: Completed by J. Brown & Company Ltd., Glasgow for Royal Mail Steam Packet Company and named LOCHKATRINE. 4.8.1932: Fleet passed into ownership of Royal Mail Lines Ltd. 3.8.1942: Torpedoed by submarine in position 45.52N, 46.44W, and subsequently sunk.

R2. LOCHGOIL (1922-1939)

ON. 146679. 9462g. 5873n. 11576d. 485.6 x 62.3 x 35.8/29.6
4SCSA. 16 cyl: $29\frac{1}{8}''-45\frac{1}{4}''$. 5000bhp. 2 screws. 13k.
12.1922: Completed by Harland & Wolff Ltd., Glasgow for Royal Mail Steam Packet Company and named LOCHGOIL. 4.8.1932: Fleet passed into ownership of Royal Mail Lines Ltd. 6.10.1939: Damaged by mine in position 51.24N, 04.00W, 4½ miles SW of Scarweather lightvessel in the Bristol Channel. Ship was towed across the channel and 7.10.1939 beached off the Mumbles lighthouse and subsequently towed into Swansea and declared a total constructive loss. Sold to the Ministry of Shipping (Royal Mail Lines Ltd., managers) and rebuilt. 1942: Renamed EMPIRE ROWAN. 27.3.1943: Torpedoed and sunk by aircraft off Philippeville in position 37.16N, 06.54W, with the loss of 3 lives.

LOCHKATRINE *Harland and Wolff*

LOCHMONAR *Harland and Wolff*

LOCHMONAR aground on Taylor's Revetment   *Furness Withy Group P.R. Dept.*

R3. LOCHMONAR (1924-1949)

ON. 147677. 9412g. 5815n. 485.6 x 62.2 x 35.5/29.6

4SCSA. 16 cyl: $29\frac{1}{8}$' – $45\frac{1}{4}$'. 5000bhp. 2 screws. 13k

7.1924: Completed by Harland & Wolff Ltd., Belfast for Royal Mail Meat Transports Ltd., and named LOCHMONAR. 30.11.1927: Following a defect developing in the steering gear LOCH-MONAR over-ran the sunken revetment at Taylor's Bank in the Mersey, and broke her back when the tide ebbed. The ship was cut in two just forward of the bridge and a new bow was fitted by the builders. LOCHMONAR's next visit to Merseyside saw the unusual spectacle of a ship passing part of herself! 4.8.1932: Fleet passed into ownership of Royal Mail Lines Ltd. 19.9.1948: Ran aground near Little Cayman Island during a hurricane. 30.9.1948: Refloated by salvage steamer "Curb". 1949: Sold to British Iron & Steel Corporation and arrived Blyth 18.4.1949 for demolition by Hughes Bolckow Ltd.

R4. ASTURIAS (1926-1946)

ON. 148146. 22071g. 12703n. 13100d. 630.5 x 78.5 x 40.5/28.7

4SCDA. 16 cyl: 33" – 59". 14000 bhp. 2 screws. 16k.

Passengers: 408 First, 200 Second, 674 Third as built
                330 First, 220 Second, 768 Third in 1934

7.1925: Launched by the Duchess of Abercorn and named ASTURIAS and 2.1926: Completed by Harland & Wolff Ltd., Belfast for Royal Mail Meat Transports Ltd. 4.8.1932: Fleet passed into ownership of Royal Mail Lines Ltd. 7.1934: Returned to builders for re-engining with Parsons S.R. Geared Turbines of 20000 shp, increasing speed to 18 knots. 9.1934: Maiden voyage as steamer. 6.1935: Attended Silver Jubilee Review at Spithead. 26.8.1939: Requisitioned for service as Armed Cruiser and commissioned 28.9.1939. 24.7.1943: Torpedoed by submarine 400 miles off Freetown while escorting a floating dock under tow, but taken in tow herself and arrived Freetown 1.8.1943, disarmed and laid up at anchor on care and maintenance. 8.2.1945: Left under tow for United Kingdom, arrived 27.2.1945, repaired and 1946: Sold to H.M. Government for service as troopship and immigrant ship. 1957: Sold to Shipbreaking Industries Ltd., and arrived Faslane 14.9.1957.

ALCANTARA (note rounded stern)   *Furness, Withy Group P.R. Dept.*

R5. ALCANTARA (1927-1958)
ON. 148151. 22181g, 13226n, 13100d. 630.5 x 78.5 x 40.5/28.7

4SCDA. 16 cyl: 33" — 59". 14000 bhp. 2 screws. 16k.
Passengers: 432 First, 200 Second, 674 Third as built
               330 First, 220 Second, 768 Third in 1934
               220 First, 185 Second, 462 Tourist in 1948

23.9.1926: Launched and named ALCANTARA and 3.1927: Completed by Harland & Wolff Ltd., for Royal Mail Meat Transports Ltd. 4.8.1932: Fleet passed into ownership of Royal Mail Lines Ltd. 11.1934: Returned to builders for re-engining with Parsons S.R. Geared Turbines of 20000 shp. Speed now 18 knots, Gross Tonnage now 22209. 4.5.1935: First voyage as a steamer. 6.1935: Attended Silver Jubilee Review at Spithead. 9.1939: Requisitioned for service as Armed Merchant Cruiser, stripped at Belfast and fitted with one 4" gun aft at Devonport. 28.9.1939: Sailed in convoy for Malta. 10.1939: Damaged in collision by SS Franconia and proceeded to Alexandria for hull repairs, arriving in Malta late 10.1939 and armed with 8 6" guns. Light A.A. gun mounted in place of fore-funnel. 28.6.1940: In action with German surface raider Thor at range of 14,000, reducing to 10,000 yards. Waterline damage sustained near engine-room and speed reduced enabling enemy to escape after sustaining some hits, repaired at Rio de Janeiro. 30.11.1943: Paid off for conversion as Troopship. 1947: Returned to Belfast for reconversion for commercial service and 8.10.1948: Re-entered service. 5.1958: Sold for £240,000 to ship-breakers and 26.6.1958 renamed KAISHO MARU and sailed for Osaka, being the first large vessel sold for breaking up in Japan since the war.

ASTURIAS   *World Ship Photo Library*

Harland and Wolff

ACHIMOTA

ELDER DEMPSTER

The Liverpool partnership that comprised Elder Dempster and Company was for the second half of the 1800's the dominant force in the West African shipping trade. For the previous 300 years the merchants of Liverpool and Bristol had master-minded the trianglular trade that included the notorious middle passage — slaves from West Africa to the Americas. If the end of slavery and the coming of steam had reformed the trade, it was still a very hostile and unhealthy area in which to run a shipping service. The flag of colonialism eventually followed the established trade patterns and British government interest grew, if somewhat reluctantly, outwards from the trade castles and compounds that dotted the coastline.

Although as close to Liverpool as the eastern Mediterranean, West Africa was still a world apart. Beyond Freetown it had not one natural harbour, and the ships carrying empire trade either worked their cargoes off surf-swept beaches into large canoes, or crept up torpid rivers with shallow bars at their mouths and jungle a hundred feet high on their banks. Malaria, rampant and then incurable, ensured that West Africa was correctly labelled the 'white man's grave', and this alone was why European settlement never became a complication of British, French and German colonial history in the area between the Sahara and the South Atlantic.

A giant of Victorian shipping dominated the West African commercial scene and consolidated Elder Dempster's role from 1884 to 1909. Alfred Jones (born 1845) came from a humble background and, starting as a cabin boy, rose rapidly to become a senior partner. A lifelong bachelor, his energies went almost entirely into the commercial development of West Africa and, parallel with developing a fleet of passenger and cargo ships, founded a bank for the West coast, developed hotels, started mines and plantations, all of which created cargoes for his ships. Almost forgotten is the fact that he put the banana on to the British table. Typical of a fascinating blend of social altruism and commercial acumen, he started the story of the banana in Britain because he was distressed by the poverty in the Canary Islands and could use a cargo that filled empty coal bunker spaces. The success of banana importing and distribution led to the founding of Elders and Fyffes and plantation development in Jamaica. So that the Lancashire cotton trade was less dependent on American cotton he encouraged its planting in Nigeria and the Caribbean but, outside shipping, Jones' most lasting triumph was the establishment of the Liverpool School of Tropical Medicine whose work to this day has consigned the term of the 'white man's grave' to history.

Sir Alfred Jones died suddenly in 1909 leaving a complicated will and only one executor with an enormous responsibility. To this hapless man Philipps and Pirrie made a comprehensive offer for the Jones estate and a deal was made extremely quickly which, on the credit side, kept Elder Dempster intact, consolidated and powerful.

None of the Kylsant companies needed the technological development offered by the diesel engine more than Elder Dempster's trade to West Africa. Anything that gave an increased cargo carrying capacity on a limited draught — 22 feet in the case of Lagos lagoon's bar — and reduced the need to carry a large amount of Welsh coal was worth putting a lot of capital into, and so it was no coincidence that ABA, as the world's first diesel engined passenger ship, operated in the African Royal Mail service. Almost immediately she was joined by a new building, the ADDA, which in fact had exactly the same hull form and layout as the pre World War One steamships ABOSSO (1913), APPAM (1913) and APAPA (1914).

With the two early motor ships a success, three more mailships were ordered, ACCRA (1926), another APAPA (1927) and finally ACHIMOTA (1929). So successful was the design for the trade that it was repeated, with modernised modifications through a further four ships up to and including the AUREOL (1951).

In many ways Philipps continued on in the grand commercial manner of Alfred Jones. His political lobbying on behalf of colonial development in West Africa resulted in some spectacular improvements in the area's port facilities and these included dockyards at Freetown and Calabar; completion of the revetment moles at Lagos; the new harbour with complete infrastructure at Takoradi, and five new berths at Apapa on Lagos lagoon. But where Jones could concentrate his talent confronting and compromising with his rivals, Philipps had neither the time nor the wisdom. In the early 1920's Elder Dempster picked a fight with one of their largest customers, the United Africa Company, who, as Lever Brothers, were huge traders in British West Africa. Strangely the core of the problem was over Elder Dempster trying to resist carrying northbound palm oil in bulk, in tanks. This led to a freight rate war and the establishment by Lever of his own fleet — which was to become Palm Line — for U.A.C. felt that the volume of their trade entitled them to a quantitative discount.

The partners of Alfred Holt showed an early interest in Elder Dempster after the collapse of the Group, not unconnected with their own interests in the Far East. Then, as now, the most valuable asset of a cargo liner company is its freight conference rights. Although Alfred Holt's Blue Funnel Line dominated the Far East trade from, and to, the U.K. west coast, they had minimal rights on the U.K. east coast and Continent. These were in the hands of Glen Line which had been bought by the Group in 1911 and shared equally between R.M.S.P. and Elder Dempster Richard (later Sir Richard) Durning Holt, the senior partner, accepted the chairmanship of Elder Dempster in March 1932 at the invitation of the Bank of England, by which time Elder Dempster were in desperate straits. The whole of their £8,485,000 capital had been lost. A ship a month was being sold to pay the wages. The ACHIMOTA was abandoned to the builders to find a buyer, the eight ships of the 'Explorer' class remained mortgaged. With £2,500,000 of new capital injected — at a time when Alfred Holts were not without problems of their own — it took until February 1935 to complete the winding up of Elder Dempster and Co. and set up Elder Dempster Lines Limited — Holts putting £750,957 into the new company, the shape of which had been masterminded by Baring Brothers. Richard Holt left the day-to-day operation of the company to Leonard Cripps, assisted by Picton Hughes Jones. In the period 1932-34, Elder Dempster sold 15 ships totalling 84,335 gross tons from a fleet which had comprised 46 ships totalling 268,516 gross tons at the time of the crash. The urgent need for a new mailship resulted in the ABOSSO (1935-1942) being ordered from Cammell Laird; and the SWEDRU (1936-1941) was the first of the five pre World War Two 'S' class all of which were direct descendants of the motorships of the 1920's. The company itself was ultimately absorbed into the Ocean Transport and Trading Group of which it remains an active member.

ADDA

A. Duncan

ABA

World Ship Photo Library

FLEET LIST

E1. ABA (1920-1947)
ON. 141887. 7374g. 4623n. 8000d. 450.5 x 55.8 x 36.6/30.5
4SCSA 16 cyl: $29\frac{1}{2}'' - 43\frac{1}{16}''$. 4800bhp. 2 screws. 14k.
360 passengers
9.1918: Completed by Barclay Curle & Co. Ltd., Glasgow for Glen Line Ltd., and named GLENAPP having been ordered for the Imperial Government of Russia, and purchased by Glen Line Ltd. whilst under construction. 1920: Purchased by British & African Steam Navigation Co. Ltd. (Elder Dempster & Co. Ltd., managers), renamed ABA and reconstructed as a passenger liner. Gross tonnage now 7937, Net tonnage 4596, Deadweight tonnage 4858, Draught 24.5'. 8.1922: Towed disabled Portuguese destroyer 'Guardiana' 422 miles to Las Palmas in severe weather. 12.1929: Steering gear damaged in severe weather and towed into Queenstown. 15.8.1932: Owners became Elder Dempster Lines Ltd. 9.1939: Requisitioned for service as Hospital Ship. 7.1.1947: Returned to owners. 29.4.1947: Sold to Bawtry Steamship Co. Ltd., London and renamed MATRONA. 31.10.1947: Capsized in Bidston Dock, Birkenhead after removal of pig iron ballast. 8.6.1948: Righted and declared total constructive loss. 4.10.1948: Sold for demolition at Barrow-in-Furness.

E2. ADDA (1922-1941)
ON. 14664. 7816g. 4663n. 6405d. 435.3 x 57.3 x 31.3/25.0
4SCSA 16 cyl: $29\frac{1}{8}' - 45\frac{1}{4}''$ 5000bhp. 2 screws. 14k.
360 passengers
11.1922: Completed by Harland & Wolff Ltd., Greenock for African Steamship Co. Ltd. (Elder Dempster & Co. Ltd., managers), and named ADDA. 15.8.1932: Owners became Elder Dempster Lines Ltd. 8.6.1941: Torpedoed and sunk by submarine off Monrovia in position 8.50N 14.39W with the loss of 12 lives.

E3. EDIBA (1923-1942)
ON 147465. 6919g. 4220n. 9190d. 406.0 x 54.2 x 32.9/27 7
4SCSA 12 cyl: $26\frac{3}{8}'' - 39\frac{3}{8}''$. 3000bhp. 2 screws. 11k.
4.1923: Completed by Harland & Wolff Ltd., Glasgow for African Steamship Co. Ltd. (Elder Dempster & Co. Ltd., managers), and named EDIBA. 9.1929: Renamed MATTAWIN. 15.8.1932: Owner became Elder Dempster Lines Ltd. 2.6.1942: Torpedoed and sunk by submarine in Long Island Sound position 40.14N, 66.01W.

29

ACCRA *A. Duncan*

E4. ACCRA (1926-1940)

ON. 149595. 9337g. 5471n. 6512d. 450.8 x 62.3 x 31.3/24.0
4SCDA 12cyl: $26\frac{3}{4}$ — $55\frac{1}{8}$". 6500bhp. 2 screws. 14k.

Passengers: 243 First, 70 Second
8.1926: Completed by Harland & Wolff Ltd., Belfast for British & African Steam Navigation Co.
Ltd. (Elder Dempster & Co. Ltd., managers), and named ACCRA. 1931: Set new record passage
11 days 21 hours Lagos — Plymouth. 15.8.1932: Owners became Elder Dempster Lines Ltd.
26.7.1940: Torpedoed and sunk by submarine S.W. of Rockall in position 55.40N, 16.28W with
the loss of 19 lives.

MATTAWIN *F. W. Hawks*

APAPA

World Ship Photo Library

E5. APAPA (1927-1940)

ON. 149611. 9333g. 5472n. 6512d. 450.7 x 62.3 x 31.3/24.0
4SCDA 12 cyl: $26\frac{3}{4}''-55\frac{1}{8}''$ 6500bhp. 2 screws. 14k.

Passengers: 243 First, 70 Second

1.1927: Completed by Harland & Wolff Ltd., Belfast for British & African Steam Navigation Co. Ltd. (Elder Dempster & Co. Ltd., managers), and named APAPA. 1931: Set new record passage Elder Dempster Lines Ltd. 15.11.1940: Bombed and sunk 200 miles S.W. of Ireland in position 54.34N, 16.47W with the loss of 23 lives.

DARU   *Ocean Archives*

E6. DUNKWA (1927-1941)

ON. 149636. 3789g. 1996n. 5870d. 355.3 x 49.2 x 22.4/22.5
4SCSA 6 cyl: $29\frac{1}{8}'' - 59\frac{1}{16}''$. 1850bhp. 10k.

8.1927: Completed by A. McMillan & Son Ltd., Dumbarton for the British & African Steam Navigation Co. Ltd. (Elder Dempster & Co. Ltd., managers), and named DUNKWA. 15.8.1932: Owners became Elder Dempster Lines Ltd. 6.5.1941: Torpedoed and sunk by submarine 216 miles W.N.W. of Freetown in position 8.49N, 16.52W with the loss of 8 lives.

DIXCOVE

F. W. Hawks

E7. DIXCOVE (1927-1941)

ON. 149641. 3790g. 1995n. 5870d. 355.4 x 49.2 x 22.4/22 7
4SCSA 6 cyl: $29\frac{1}{8}'' - 59\frac{1}{16}''$. 1850bhp. 10k.

10.1927: Completed by A. McMillan & Son Ltd., Dumbarton for the British & African Steam Navigation Co. Ltd. (Elder Dempster & Co. Ltd., managers), and named DIXCOVE. 15.8.1932: Owners became Elder Dempster Lines Ltd. 24.9.1941: Torpedoed and sunk by submarine N.W. of Canary Islands in position 31.12N, 23.41W with the loss of 1 life.

E8. DARU (1927-1941)

ON. 149652. 3839g. 2106n. 5870d. 355.4 x 49.2 x 22.4/22.7
4SCSA 6 cyl: $29\frac{1}{8}'' - 59\frac{1}{16}''$. 1850bhp. 10k.

12.1927: Completed by A. McMillan & Son Ltd., Dumbarton for the British & African Steam Navigation Co. Ltd. (Elder Dempster & Co. Ltd., managers), and named DARU. 15.8.1932: Owners became Elder Dempster Lines Ltd. 15.9.1941: Bombed and sunk in Bristol Channel in position 51.56N, 0.58W.

DAGOMBA laid up at Dartmouth *F. W. Hawks*

E9. DAGOMBA (1928-1942)

ON. 149669. 3845g. 2100n. 5870d. 355.3 x 49.2 x 22.4/22.5
4SCSA 6 cyl: $29\frac{1}{8}''-59\frac{1}{16}''$. 1850bhp. 10k.

3.1928: Completed by A. McMillan & Son Ltd., Dumbarton for the British & African Steam Navigation Co. Ltd. (Elder Dempster & Co. Ltd., Managers), and named DAGOMBA. 15.8.1932: Owners became Elder Dempster Lines Ltd. 3.11.1942: Torpedoed and sunk by submarine 450 miles W. of Freetown in position 02.29N, 0.19W with the loss of 7 lives.

E10. DEIDO (1928-1959)

ON. 160370. 3878g. 2122n. 5851d. 356.6 x 49.2 x 22.4/22.5
4SCSA 6 cyl: $29\frac{1}{8}''-59\frac{1}{16}'$. 1850bhp. 10k.

3.1928: Completed by Ardrossan Drydock and Shipbuilding Co. Ltd., Ardrossan for African Steamship Co. Ltd. (Elder Dempster & Co. Ltd., managers), and named DEIDO. 15.8.1932: Owners became Elder Dempster Lines Ltd. 9.1958: Sold to Eckhardt & Co., Hamburg for demolition.

The uneventful life recorded above omits mention of a distinctly eventful birth in the form of protracted labour pains at launching. The launch took place in winter and after the naming ceremony DEIDO deigned to move at a rate of 1/8th inch every few minutes down a slipway of declivity 5/8" to 1'. The combined efforts of all shipyard employees pushing made no apparent difference. Unfortunately, as the tide was receding rather faster the problem was transformed into how to stop DEIDO ending up on a hard concrete berth, eventually resolved by reinsertion of the discarded keel and bilge blocks.

Blame was attributed to the tallow freezing on the slip, so after lighting flares another equally unsuccessful attempt was made the next morning. Finally DEIDO, almost renamed DO OR DIE, went afloat under the guidance of two hydraulic rams.

As can be seen, once afloat DEIDO kept it that way. Her 4 sisters, all launched at the first attempt, became war losses!

DEIDO as built. Note the short funnel, subsequently lengthened *World Ship Photo Library*

MILVERTON *F. W. Hawks*

E11. MILVERTON (1928-1934)
See GLENTARA G9

E12. KWAIBO (1928-1941)

ON. 161061. 396g. 203n. 157.5 x 26.1 x 9.3

2SCSA 8 cyl: $11\frac{13}{16}''$ — $12\frac{13}{16}''$ by J. & C. G. Bolinders Co. Ltd. Stockholm. 500bhp. 2 screws. 8k

1928: Completed by J. Crichton & Co. Ltd., Saltney for Nigerian Transport Co. Ltd. (Elder Dempster & Co. Ltd., managers), and named KWAIBO. 15.8.1932: Owners became Elder Dempster Lines Ltd. 1.8.1942: Stranded on Kwaibo Bar, Eket and became a total loss.

KWAIBO *Clwyd County Record Office*

DAVID LIVINGSTONE *World Ship Photo Library*

E13. DAVID LIVINGSTONE (1930-1953)

ON. 161146. 4022g. 2175n. 5860d. 370.6 x 51.6 x 20.1/22.5

4SCSA 8 cyl: $29\frac{1}{8}''$ — $59\frac{1}{16}''$. 4250bhp. 13k.

4.1930: Completed by A. McMillan & Son Ltd., Dumbarton for British & African Steam Navigation Co. Ltd. (Elder Dempster & Co Ltd., managers), and named DAVID LIVINGSTONE. 15.8. 1932: Owners became Elder Dempster Ltd. Ltd 1953: Sold to British Iron & Steel Corp. and arrived at T. W. Ward Ltd., Grays, Essex, 11.9. 1953 for demolition

E14. HENRY STANLEY (1930-1942)

ON. 161382. 4028g. 2188n. 5650d. 370.5 x 51.6 x 20.1/22.6

4SCSA 8 cyl: $29\frac{1}{8}'' - 59\frac{1}{16}'$. 4250bhp. 13k.

4.1930: Completed by Ardrossan Dockyard Co. Ltd. Ardrossan for African Steamship Co. Ltd. (Elder Dempster & Co. Ltd. managers) and named HENRY STANLEY. 15.8.1932: Owners became Elder Dempster Lines Ltd. 7.12.1942: Torpedoed and sunk by submarine 580 miles W. of Fayal (Azores) in position 48.50N, 39.30W with the loss of 64 lives in the severe weather prevailing.

HENRY STANLEY   *F. W. Hawks*

E.15 EDWARD BLYDEN (1930-1941)

ON. 161156. 4022g. 2155n. 5860d. 370.6 x 51.6 x 20.1/22.5

4SCSA 8 cyl: $29\frac{1}{8}'' - 59\frac{1}{16}'$. 4250bhp. 13k.

6.1930: Completed by Harland & Wolff Ltd., Govan for British & African Steam Navigation Co. Ltd. (Elder Dempster & Co. Ltd., managers), and named EDWARD BLYDEN 15.8.1932. Owners became Elder Dempster Lines Ltd. 22.9.1941: Torpedoed and sunk by U103 700 miles W. of Canary Islands in position 27.36N, 24.39W.

MARY KINGSLEY   *World Ship Photo Library*

E16. MARY KINGSLEY (1930-1954)

ON. 162510. 4017g. 2175n. 5650d. 370.5 x 51.6 x 20.1/22.5

4SCSA 8 cyl: $29\frac{1}{8}'' - 59\frac{1}{16}''$ by J. & G. Kincaid, Glasgow. 4250bhp. 13k.

1930: Completed by Ardrossan Dockyard Co. Ltd., Ardrossan for African Steamship Co. Ltd. (Elder Dempster & Co. Ltd., managers), and named MARY KINGSLEY. 15.8.1932: Owners became Elder Dempster Lines Ltd. 9.1954: Sold to British Iron & Steel Corp., and arrived T. W. Ward Ltd., Preston 18.9.1954 for demolition.

MARY SLESSOR *World Ship Photo Library*

E17. MARY SLESSOR (1930-1943)

ON. 161149. 4016g. 2163n. 5650d. 370.6 × 51.6 × 20.1/22.5
4SCSA 8 cyl: $29\frac{1}{8}$" − $59\frac{1}{16}$". 4250bhp. 13k.
5.1930: Completed by A. McMillan & Son Ltd., Dumbarton for British & African Steam Navigation Co. Ltd., (Elder Dempster & Co. Ltd., managers) and named MARY SLESSOR. 15.8.1932: Owners became Elder Dempster Lines Ltd. 7.2.1943: Mined at 23.58 hours off Gibraltar in position 35.55N, 6.02W and sank in under 15 minutes with the loss of 32 lives.

WILLIAM WILBERFORCE *F. W. Hawks*

E.18. WILLIAM WILBERFORCE (1930-1943)

ON. 161406. 4013g. 2165n. 5650d. 370.2 x 51.7 x 20.1/22.5
4SCSA 8 cyl: $29\frac{1}{8}''-59\frac{1}{16}''$. 4250bhp. 13k.
5.1930: Completed by D. & W. Henderson Ltd., Glasgow for African Steamship Co. Ltd. (Elder
Dempster & Co. Ltd., managers) and named WILLIAM WILBERFORCE. 15.8.1932: Owners
became Elder Dempster Lines Ltd. 9.1.1943: Torpedoed and sunk in position 29.20N, 26.53W
with the loss of 3 lives.

MACGREGOR LAIRD
F. W. Hawks

E19. MACGREGOR LAIRD (1930-1953)

ON. 161450. 4015g. 2167n. 5650d. 370.1 x 51.7 x 20.1/22.5
4SCSA 8 cyl: $29\frac{1}{8}''-59\frac{1}{16}''$. 4250bhp. 13k.
7.1930: Completed by D. & W. Henderson, Glasgow for African Steamship Co. Ltd. (Elder
Dempster & Co. Ltd., managers), and named MACGREGOR LAIRD. 15.8.1932: Owners became
Elder Dempster Lines Ltd. 1953: Sold to Anglo-Saxon Petroleum Co. Ltd., for use as a depot
ship and named SHELL QUEST. 1954: Transferred to Shell Co. of Qatar Ltd., London, name
unchanged. 1956: Sold to Stanhal Navigation, Costa Rica and renamed SALAMAT. 10.1961:
Broken up in Yugoslavia.

E20. ALFRED JONES (1930-1941)

ON. 162322. 4022g. 2155n. 5860d. 370.6 x 51.6 x 20.1/22.6
4SCSA 8 cyl: $29\frac{1}{8}''-59\frac{1}{16}''$. 4250bhp. 13k.
9.1930: Completed by Harland & Wolff Ltd., Glasgow for British & African Steam Navigation
Co. Ltd. (Elder Dempster & Co. Ltd., managers), and named ALFRED JONES. 15.8.1932: Owners
became Elder Dempster Lines Ltd. 1.6.1941: Torpedoed and sunk by sumbarine 18 miles W. of
Freetown in position 8N, 15W, approximately, with the loss of 2 lives.

E21. ACHIMOTA

ON. 153950. 9576g. 5625n. 6238d. 461.2 x 63.9 x 29.1/24.5

4SCSA 16 cyl: $29\frac{1}{8}''-59\frac{1}{16}''$. 8500bhp. 2 screws. 15k.

9.1931: Completed by Harland & Wolff Ltd., Belfast to the order of British & African Steam Navigation Co. Ltd. (Elder Dempster & Co. Ltd., managers), and named ACHIMOTA but delivery not taken owing to owners being unable to meet the final instalments of the purchase price. 9.1932: Sold to Huddart Parker Ltd., Melbourne, refitted and renamed WANGANELLA and arrived Melbourne 12.1932. 5.1941: Requisitioned for service as Hospital Ship by the Australian Government. 14.4.1944: At Bombay when S.S. 'Fort Stikine' blew up and acted as emergency operating theatre and casualty station. 1946: Returned to owners and refitted. Gross tonnage now 9876, Net tonnage 5741. 19.1.1947: Struck the Barrett Reef at the entrance to Wellington Harbour. 6.2.1947: Refloated and 18.2.1947 entered the Floating Dock for immediate repairs. 10.1948: Completed repairs and re-entered service. 9.1961: Owners sold to McIlwraith McEacharn, Melbourne, name unchanged. 4.1962: Sold to Hang Fung Shipping Co., Hong Kong, name unchanged. 1963: Sold to New Zealand Government to act as floating hostel for contractors engaged on Manapouri hydro-electric scheme and moored at Deep Cove, Doubtful Sound. 12.1969: Sold to Australian Pacific Shipping Co., Hong Kong. 1970: Towed to Hong Kong and broken up.

ALFRED JONES   *F. W. Hawks*

REINA DEL PACÍFICO

PACIFIC STEAM NAVIGATION COMPANY

There had been a long link between P.S.N.C. and Royal Mail. In 1835 the Government of Chile granted an American trader, William Wheelright, a ten year monopoly to operate a coastal service with steam paddle ships. Significantly, he could not raise the capital in the United States but found London more imaginative and even secured a Royal Charter in 1839. With new, British built, ships the service started in 1840 and soon extended northwards to operate between Valparaiso to Panama connecting by the 'Panama Overland' with Royal Mail's U.K. — Caribbean service; this became supported by mail subsidies both from the British Government and those of Peru, Bolivia (which until a local war in 1879-83 had Pacific Ocean frontage) and Chile.

A mining boom in the 1870's resulted in P.S.N.C. opening a direct service between the U.K. and Chile through the Straits of Magellan. In 1873 P.S.N.C., with 19 ships, was the largest steamship owner in the world. The prosperity of Chile attracted numerous other owners leading to massive over exploitation of the trade. With as many as 11 of P.S.N.C's ships laid up, desperation led to 4 vessels being chartered to the newly formed Orient Line for their service to Australia. This co-operation worked well, each company using the other's surplus passenger-cargo tonnage to the extent that there was even a common prefix 'OR' until 1906 when the P.S.N.C. ships used in the Australian trade and its connections were sold to R.M.S.P.

Around the turn of the century Argentina overtook Chile as the dominant economic power in the temperate part of South America. British investment was opening up the rich interior of Argentina, while South Africa slowly recovered from the Boer War and Australia suffered from a succession of blasting droughts. The completion of the Trans-Andean railway in 1910 and progress on cutting the canal at Panama meant that P.S.N.C. were facing massive changes. Owen Philipps, already a substantial shareholder, drew the threads of trading circumstances together and acquired P.S.N.C. for the R.M.S.P., although it continued to run independently from Liverpool.

The Panama Canal opened on 15 August 1914 and had a profound effect on the trading pattern of the South American Pacific litoral. The 'Straits' service was abandoned by P.S.N.C.; the United States, both as a source of supplies and as a market, was brought nearer by thousands of miles; finally, far reaching flag preference laws drastically affected P.S.N.C.'s involvement in Chile after 1920.

In 1912 R.M.S.P. had introduced 4 of the second group of 'A' Class 15,000 tonners to the U.K. — River Plate trade. These were followed by 3 modified versions for P.S.N.C.; they were ORDUNA (1914-1951), ORBITA (1915-1950) and the ORCA (1918-1935). In the post World War One period, with their own trade curtailed, P.S.N.C.'s passenger-carrying ships —which also included 5 older ships — were completely sublimated to the needs of the Group with various ships being taken off for periods of service with White Star and Royal Mail, while the new 'L' Class motor ships carried the general cargo. The promise of the Pacific trade led to the building and commissioning of the REINA DEL PACIFICO but by the time she sailed on her maiden voyage on 9 April 1931 the Group was near to demise. Furness Withy, masterminded by Lord Essenden, acquired Royal Mail after the realisation, and eventually P.S.N.C. in 1938. The success of the 'L' Class inspired confidence to build the 'S' Class during World War Two, and after a prolonged gestation period REINA DEL PACIFICO's successor REINA DEL MAR appeared to serve the West Coast route from 1956 to 1963, after which, badly affected by Castro's conquest of Cuba, she was chartered by, and later sold to, Union-Castle as a successful full time cruise ship until she succumbed to rising oil prices in 1975. Today P.S.N.C. continues to operate a small fleet of cargo liners.

FLEET LIST

P1. LA PAZ (1920-1942)

ON. 143671. 6548g. 4052n. 9190d. 406.3 x 54.2 x 32.9/27.0
4SCSA 12 cyl: $26\frac{3}{8}''$ — $39\frac{3}{8}''$. 3000bhp. 2 screws. 11k.

10.1920: Completed by Harland & Wolff Ltd., Glasgow for Pacific Steam Navigation Co. Ltd. and named LA PAZ. 1.5.1942: Damaged by submarine torpedo off Florida in position 28.15N, 80.20W and taken over by United States War Shipping Administration, Jacksonville. 1946: Sold to Construction Aggregates Corp., Jacksonville, name unchanged. 1947: Sold to Armament H. Vervliet, Antwerp and renamed RUBENS. 7.1951: Caught fire and ran aground S. of Tokyo, refloated 23.7.1951 but sank shortly afterwards.

LOBOS

Harland and Wolff

LA PAZ

Furness Withy Group P.R. Dept.

P2. LOBOS (1921-1952)
ON. 145879. 6479g. 3997n. 9190d. 405.6 x 54.2 x 32.8/27.0
4SCSA 12 cyl: $26\frac{3}{8}'' - 39\frac{3}{8}''$. 3000bhp. 2 screws. 11k.
10.1921: Completed by Harland & Wolff Ltd., Greenock for Pacific Steam Navigation Co. Ltd., and named LOBOS. 11.7.1952: Arrived at Inverkeithing for breaking up by T. W. Ward.

LOSADA   *World Ship Photo Library*

P3. LOSADA (1921-1952)
ON. 145888. 6520g. 4021n. 9190d. 406.1 x 54.2 x 32.8/27.0
4SCSA 12 cyl: $26\frac{3}{8}'' - 39\frac{3}{8}''$. 3000bhp. 2 screws. 11k.
10.1921: Completed by Harland & Wolff Ltd., Glasgow for Pacific Steam Navigation Co. Ltd., and named LOSADA. 26.10.1952: Sold to T. W. Ward and arrived at Barrow for breaking up.

LAGUNA   *Furness Withy Group P.R. Dept.*

P4. LAGUNA (1923-1952)
ON. 147226. 6469g. 4033n. 9310d. 420.5 x 54.2 x 33.3/28.2
4SCSA 12 cyl: $26\frac{3}{4}'' - 43\frac{5}{16}''$. 3300bhp. 2 screws. 11k.
7.1923: Completed by Harland & Wolff Ltd., Glasgow for Pacific Steam Navigation Co. Ltd. and named LAGUNA. 24.8.1952: Sold to T. W. Ward and arrived at Barrow for breaking up.

LAGARTO   *A. Duncan*

P5. LAGARTO (1923-1948)
See GLENAVY G4

P6. LAUTARO (1923-1946)
See GLENGYLE G2

P7. LORETO (1923-1951)
See GLENADE G6

P8. LORIGA (1923-1951)
See GLENARIFFF G7

LORETO   *World Ship Photo Library*

P9. REINA DEL PACIFICO (1931-1958)

ON. 162339. 17707g. 10745n. 9990d. 551.3 x 76.3 x 37.8/31.2
4SCSA 48 cyl: $24\frac{13}{16}$" — $47\frac{1}{4}$". 22000bhp. 4 screws. 18½k.

Passengers: 280 First, 162 Second, 466 Third as built
257 First, 151 Second, 334 Third in 1948

3.1931: Completed by Harland & Wolff Ltd., Belfast for Pacific Steam Navigation Co. Ltd., and named REINA DEL PACIFICO. 9.4.1931: Sailed on maiden voyage from Liverpool to Valparaiso. 21.10.1936: Arrived at Liverpool after record 25 day passage from Valparaiso. 8.1939: Requisitioned for service as troopship. 8.1942: Converted to Landing Assault Ship. 1946: Returned to builders for reconstruction. 11.9.1947: Explosion in crankcase while on trials resulted in death of 23 engine-room personnel. 1948: Re-entered service, Gross tonnage now 17872, Net tonnage 10402. 8.7.1957: Ran aground on Devil's Flat off Bermuda. 11.7.1957: Refloated after discharging 700 tons cargo with no damage, and 14.7.1957 resumed voyage. 5.1958: Sold for breaking up and delivered to John Cashmore Ltd., Newport.

REINA DEL PACIFICO another view of the engine room *Harland & Wolff*

GLENOGLE

GLEN LINE

The early days of Glen Line are centred around two Scottish families, the McGregors and the Gows. Both from humble Highland origins, they set up shipbroking and cargo trading businesses in Glasgow in the mid 1800's, and their parallel histories drew them together. Both families' interest in the advancing technology of shipbuilding encouraged its development on the banks of the Clyde; this was in the form of the London and Glasgow Engineering and Iron Ship Building Company Limited which, by an odd quirk of history, was to become Harland & Wolff's Clydeside yard.

James McGregor, having built two sailing ships, was amongst the first to appreciate that the opening of the Suez Canal in November 1869 would give steamships a huge commercial advantage over sailing ships in both the Indian and Far Eastern trades and so the GLENGYLE (1600 GRT) made her maiden voyage in November 1870 to Madras and Calcutta. She returned to London in July 1871 having made a gross dividend of 30% on the voyage. In 1874 the McGregor and the Gow firms merged, and as a result moved into the Far East — New York trade and eventually into the premium-rated tea trade — a seasonal one — from China to the U.K.

The tea clippers' races were superseded by steamships with some incredible (for the day) times being set against a setting of intense commercial rivalry. The main rival to Glen Line was Thomas Skinner, another Glasgow owner. As an example, in 1877 Skinner's LOUDON CASTLE passed Woosung on 25 May at the same time as the GLENEAGLES and they arrived at London within 24 hours of each other on 3 and 4 July respectively. By 1881 the GLENOGLE was achieving a homeward average speed of 15 knots but this was gained by a fuel consumption of 110 tons of coal a day whilst Alfred Holt's much more staid approach to the China trade had steamships doing 9 knots on 20 tons a day.

Aside from the glamour of the tea races the commercial hard-headedness of the Scots had helped with the foundation of the first freight 'conference' in 1879. By 1890 the China tea trade had been made extinct and new, larger, economical ships were being built for changed trading conditions and operating a fortnightly service based on London. In 1911 Elder Dempster, who themselves had joined the Group in 1910, acquired a controlling interest. This resulted in the amalgamation of Royal Mail's small Shire Line with Glen Line in 1920.

The McGregors' interest in technological development undoubtedly led to the company's interest in diesel-engined ships, and the GLENGYLE followed by GLENAPP as Britain's pioneering of large motor ships.

Well established in a well paying trade, Glen Line had a dominant role in the U.K. and North Continent to China trade. They concentrated their efforts on Shanghai and the North China ports. The terms of R.M.S.P. suzerainty were exacting. A fixed dividend of 5% was paid (in an era when the bank rate was established at 2%) plus a commission of ½% of the gross revenue. In seven of the eight years 1920-27 the minimum dividend was paid but at a cost of over £5M out of reserves. In common with so many of the Group's member companies all the ordinary shareholders' capital was lost. Glen Line was acquired by Alfred Holt and the old rivalry was eliminated in 1935.

Although Holts had experimented with diesel engined ships since building the TANTALUS in 1923, they were still hedging their bets by building coal-burners in 1925. Almost as soon as the takeover was completed, Alfred Holts designed a new class of 10,000 ton, 18 knot, twin screw motor ships. This was the GLENROY Class of which six were delivered and in service before the outbreak of World War Two in September 1939. They were brilliantly successful ships and with a return to peacetime trading made substantial profits. Further modern vessels were added in the 1960's but the development of container transport and its application to the Far East routes resulted in the disappearance of the Glen Line houseflag a decade later.

G1. GLENARTNEY (1915-1918)

ON. 137812. 7263g. 4599n. 10160d. 435.9 x 55.3 x 35.2/29.2

4SCSA 12 cyl: $26\frac{3}{8}''-39\frac{3}{8}''$. 2600bhp. 2 screws. $10\frac{1}{2}$k.

9.1915: Completed by Harland & Wolff Ltd., Irvine for Glen Line Ltd., and named GLENARTNEY
5.2.1918: Torpedoed and sunk by submarine 30 miles N.E. of Cape Bon with the loss of 2 lives.

G2. GLENGYLE (1915-1923)

ON. 137487. 6240g. 3950n. 9550d. 399.1 x 52.2 x 33.9/28.9

4SCSA 12 cyl: $24\frac{13}{16}''-33\frac{1}{2}''$. 2300bhp. 2 screws. $10\frac{1}{2}$k.

12.1915: Completed by Harland & Wolff Ltd., Glasgow for Glen Line Ltd., and named GLENGYLE, having been purchased on the stocks from F. Leyland & Co. Ltd., original name BOSTONIAN. 1923: Transferred to Pacific Steam Navigation Co. Ltd., and renamed LAUTARO. 1946: Sold to Jenny Steamship Co. Ltd. (G. J. Livanos, manager), London, Panamanian Flag and renamed RIVER SWIFT. 7.1948: Damaged by fire and explosion in Rio de Janeiro and broken up.

GLENAMOY   *Ocean Archives*

G3. GLENAMOY (1916-1936)

ON. 137826 7269g. 4656n. 10160d. 436.0 x 55.3 x 35.2/29.2

4SCSA 12 cyl: $26\frac{3}{8}''-39\frac{3}{8}''$. 2600bhp. 2 screws. $10\frac{1}{2}$k.

10.1916: Completed by Harland & Wolff Ltd., Irvine for Glen Line Ltd., and named GLENAMOY.
11.7.1936: Sold for breaking up by Metal Industries and arrived Rosyth.

G4. GLENAVY (1917-1923)

ON. 137855. 5075g, 3208n, 7520d. 385.1 x 52.2 x 30.3/26.7

4SCSA 12 cyl: $24\frac{13}{16}''-33\frac{1}{2}''$. 2300bhp. 2 screws. $10\frac{1}{2}$k.

9.1917: Completed by Harland & Wolff Ltd., Glasgow for Glen Line Ltd., and named GLENAVY. 1923: Transferred to Pacific Steam Navigation Co. Ltd., and renamed LAGARTO. 26.9.1948: Sold to Cochrane and arrived at Troon for breaking up.

G5. GLENAPP I (1918-1920)

See ABA E1

GLENADE　　　　　　　　　　　　　　　　　　　　*F. W. Hawks*

G6.　GLENADE (1919-1923)

ON. 141913. 6275g. 4105n. 9090d. 406.2 x 54.2 x 23.6/26.9

4SCSA 12 cyl: $26\frac{3}{8}''-39\frac{3}{8}''$. 2600bhp. 2 screws. 10½k.

7.1919: Completed by Harland & Wolff Ltd., Glasgow for Glen Line Ltd., and named GLENADE. 1923: Transferred to Pacific Steam Navigation Co. Ltd., and renamed LORETTO. 1951: Sold to Motor Lines Ltd., Greenock and renamed BARBETA. 11.1952: Sold to British Iron & Steel Corp., and arrived 21.11.1952 at Briton Ferry for breaking up.

G7.　GLENARIFFE (1919-1923)

ON. 141927. 6665g. 4951n. 9030d. 406.0 x 54.2 x 23.6/27.0

4SCSA 12 cyl: $29\frac{1}{8}''-39\frac{3}{8}''$. 2600bhp. 2 screws. 10½k.

10.1919: Completed by Harland & Wolff Ltd., Glasgow for Glen Line Ltd., and named GLENARIFFE. 1923: Transferred to Pacific Steam Navigation Co. Ltd., and renamed LORIGA. 1951: Sold to Audax Shipping Co. Ltd., Hong Kong and renamed OCEAN VENUS. 1953: Broken up in Japan.

GLENLUCE　　　　　　　　　　　　　　　　　　*Ocean Archives*

G8.　GLENLUCE (1920-1936)

ON. 141941. 6755g. 4120n. 9030d. 405.9 x 54.2 x 32.9/27.0

4SCSA 12 cyl: $26\frac{3}{8}''-39\frac{3}{8}''$. 2600bhp. 2 screws. 10½k.

1.1920: Completed by Harland & Wolff Ltd., Glasgow for Glen Line Ltd., and named GLENLUCE 2.1936: Sold to P. Wigham Richardson & Co., and renamed IONOPOLIS and handed over 5.1936. 1937: Sold to Skibs A/S Vigrid, Tonsberg (Bruum and von der Lippe, managers), and renamed VIGEO. 1938: Sold to Rederi A/B Jamaica & Stockholm (Sven Salen, manager), and renamed KORSHAMN. Gross Tonnage now 6683, Net tonnage 4057. 17.3.1941: Torpedoed and sunk by submarine while on passage Halifax to Liverpool. 11 survivors subsequently rescued.

G9. GLENTARA (1920-1928)
ON. 144193. 6754g. 4123n. 9030d. 406.0 x 54.2 x 32.9/27.0

4SCSA 12 cyl: $26\frac{3}{8}''$ — $39\frac{3}{8}''$. 2600bhp. 2 screws. 10½k.

1920: Completed by Harland & Wolff Ltd., Glasgow for Glen Line Ltd., and named GLENTARA.
1928: Transferred to British & African Steam Navigation Company Ltd. (Elder Dempster & Co. Ltd., managers). and renamed MILVERTON. 15.8.1932: Owner became Elder Dempster Lines Ltd. 5.1934: Sold to W. R. Carpenter & Co., Suva and renamed SALAMAUA. Owner subsequently became W. R. Carpenter Overseas Shipping Ltd. 1947: Sold to Pacific Shipowners Ltd., Suva and 1948 Renamed LAUTOKA. 7.1953: Broken up in Japan.

G10. GLENOGLE (1920-1949)
ON. 144217. 9513g. 5880n. 12300d. 485.8 x 62.3 x 35.8/29.5

4SCSA 16 cyl: $29\frac{1}{8}''$ — $45\frac{1}{4}''$. 4500bhp. 2 screws. 12½k.

8.1920: Completed by Harland & Wolff Ltd., Glasgow for Glen Line Ltd., and named GLENOGLE.
4.1949: Transferred to Blue Funnel Line and named DEUCALION. 3.1956: Sold to British Iron & Steel Co., and broken up at Briton Ferry by T. W. Ward Ltd., arrived 11.3.1956.

GLENAPP II

A. Duncan

G11. GLENAPP II (1920-1949)
ON. 144230. 9503g. 5877n. 12300d. 485.6 x 62.3 x 35.8/29.5

4SCSA 16 cyl: $29\frac{1}{8}''$ — $45\frac{1}{4}''$. 4500bhp. 2 screws. 12½k.

12.1920: Completed by Harland & Wolff Ltd., Glasgow for Glen Line Ltd., and named GLENAPP.
1.1949: Transferred to Blue Funnel Line and renamed DARDANUS. 7.1957: Sold to British Iron & Steel Co., and broken up at Inverkeithing by T. W. Ward Ltd., arrived 19.7.1957.

G12. GLENGARRY (1922-1949)
ON. 146283. 9460g. 5843n. 12300d. 485.6 x 62.3 x 35.8/29.5

4SCSA 16 cyl: $29\frac{1}{8}''$ — $45\frac{1}{4}''$. 4500bhp. 2 screws. 12½k.

2.1922: Completed by Harland & Wolff, Glasgow for Glen Line Ltd., and named GLENGARRY.
1939: Renamed GLENSTRAE. 2.1949: Transferred to Blue Funnel Line and renamed DOLIUS.
8.1952: Damaged tailshaft whilst docking at Liverpool. Sold to T. W. Ward Ltd., and arrived Briton Ferry 20.8.1952 for breaking up.

GLENBEG

G13. GLENBEG (1922-1949)
ON. 146292. 9461g. 5846n. 12300d. 485.6 x 62.3 x 35.8/29.6
4SCSA 16 cyl: $29\frac{1}{8}''-45\frac{1}{4}''$. 4500bhp. 2 screws. 12½k.
4.1922: Completed by Harland & Wolff Ltd., Glasgow for Glen Line Ltd., and named GLENBEG.
8.1949: Transferred to Blue Funnel Line and renamed DYMAS. 4.1954: Sold to British Iron &
Steel Co., and broken up at Dalmuir by W. H. Arnott Young & Co. Ltd., arrived 8.4.1954 and
hulk towed 3.8.1954 to Old Kilpatrick for demolition.

GLENSHIEL

G14. GLENSHIEL (1924-1942)
ON. 145439. 9415g. 5803n. 12065d. 485.7 x 62.2 x 35.5
4SCSA 16 cyl: $29\frac{1}{8}''-45\frac{1}{4}''$. 4500bhp. 2 screws. 12½k.
5.1924: Completed by Harland & Wolff Ltd., Belfast for Glen Line Ltd., and named GLENSHIEL.
2.4.1942: Torpedoed and subk by Japanese submarine 300 miles E. of Maldives in position 01.00S,
78.11E whilst on voyage Colombo — Fremantle.

LASSELL

LAMPORT AND HOLT LINE

Lamport and Holt originated in a partnership entered into by William Lamport and George Holt, brother of Alfred Holt, founder of the Blue Funnel Line.

The business started with a fleet of small wooden sailing vessels trading between Liverpool and North America, South America, and South Africa. The line bought its first steamship in 1857 and, after 4 years' satisfactory experience, more were ordered.

A regular service to Brazil and the River Plate commenced in 1863 following pressure brought upon the partners by Alfred and Phillip Holt, and this soon evolved into the company's principal interest.

Until 1902 Lamport and Holt were solely concerned with cargo but in that year two fairly new ships were bought from Furness, Withy and Company and employed in a new passenger service between New York and the Plate with sufficient success to justify orders for three larger and faster successors shortly before the outbreak of the First World War. By this time the company had expanded to such an extent that it was converted into a public company, and in 1912 became a member of the Kylsant Group.

After the end of the War two new cargo steamers of 7,400 tons were ordered. They entered service in 1920 and in that year three diesel powered sisters were ordered from the company's subsidiary yard, A. McMillan & Co. of Dumbarton.

The three motorships appeared to be successful in service but conclusive proof that they were superior to their steam powered predecessors is lacking as no further orders were placed for many years afterwards. Lamport and Holt were among the harder hit of the Group members and the appointment of a Receiver in August 1930 was the beginning of a difficult decade. Most of the line's foreign investments were sold, including their shareholding in the Argentine Navigation Company, and also 20 of the fleet of 41 ships. Reconstruction in 1934 involved sale of the assets of Lamport and Holt Ltd. to the associated Liverpool, Brazil, and River Plate Steam Navigation Company Ltd., which thereupon changed its name to Lamport and Holt Ltd. Only then could new construction be planned, three motorships of ultra-modern streamlined appearance. In June 1944 the line was acquired by its erstwhile rivals Blue Star Line but continued to trade under its own colours and in 1983 unlike so many of its fellow Group members, still operated a fleet of 4 modern ships.

An illustration of the appalling circumstances ruling during the depression and period of Receivership is afforded by the example of m.v. LASSELL which in March 1932 docked at Liverpool from South America manned entirely by certificated officers, those acting as deck hands and as oilers being paid as such.

LEIGHTON   *World Ship Photo Library*

L1. LEIGHTON (1921-1946)

ON. 145877. 7412g. 4485n. 1049d. 430.1 x 56.2 x 34.9/28.6

4SCSA 12 cyl: $26\frac{3}{8}''-39\frac{3}{8}''$. 3000bhp. 2 screws. 10½k.

10.1921: Completed by A. McMillan & Son Ltd., Dumbarton for Liverpoll Brazil & River Plate Steam Navigation Co. Ltd. and named LEIGHTON. 1934: Owners reconstructed and renamed Lamport & Holt Line Ltd. 28.8.1946: Sold to Smith & Houston Ltd., Port Glasgow for breaking up but requisitioned by Admiralty and 9.8.1947: loaded with gas bombs and scuttled in the North Atlantic 100 miles NW of Malin Head.

LINNELL   *W. Lind Collection, Glasgow University Archives*

L2. LINNELL (1921-1939)

ON. 145900. 7424g. 4494n. 10500d. 430.0 x 56.2 x 34.9/28.6

4SCSA 12 cyl: $26\frac{3}{4}''-43\frac{5}{16}''$. 3250bhp. 2 screws. 11k.

12.1921: Completed by A. McMillan & Son Ltd., Dumbarton for Liverpool Brazil & River Plate Steam Navigation Co. Ltd. and named LINNELL. 1934: Owners reconstructed and renamed Lamport & Holt Line Ltd. 1939: Stranded at Alexandria but refloated badly damaged, and sold for breaking up. 23.8.1939: Arrived Troon.

L3. LASSELL (1922-1941)

ON. 145939. 7417g. 4491n. 10400d. 430.2 x 56.2 x 34.9/28.6

4SCSA 12 cyl: $26\frac{3}{4}''-43\frac{5}{16}''$. 3250bhp. 2 screws. 11k.

6.1922: Completed by A. McMillan & Son Ltd., Dumbarton for Liverpool Brazil & River Plate Steam Navigation Co. Ltd. and named LASSELL. 1934: Owners reconstructed and renamed Lamport & Holt Line Ltd. 30.4.1941: Torpedoed and sunk by submarine in position 12.55N, 28.56W, 15 lives lost. The Chief Officer's boat with its 26 men aboard was picked up 10 days later by the Elder Dempster Line's "Egba". There appears to be some doubt as to whether the submarine responsible was U22 or U107.

CARNARVON CASTLE. Launching   *Harland and Wolff*

WINCHESTER CASTLE. The 'Baronial Hall' style First Class Lounge *Union-Castle Line*

UNION-CASTLE LINE

The links between Royal Mail and Union-Castle originate from the earliest days, for Captain Mangles of the R.M.S.P. was one of the first directors of the Southampton Steam Shipping Company, formed in 1853 by a number of businessmen and actively promoted by P. & O. Line and the R.M.S.P. to carry coal from the South Wales coal-fields to Southampton for their ocean mail steamers. The name was almost immediately changed to Union Steam Collier Company Ltd. and a small fleet ordered, but only a couple of voyages were made in the intended trade before the exigencies of the Crimean War caused the colliers to be taken up as transports, or by the two mail companies as replacements for their requisitioned tonnage. By the time that hostilities ceased the coal trade was adequately catered for and the company, now Union Steamship Company Ltd. was seeking ways of employing its ships. After a year of setbacks the contract for carrying the Royal Mails to Cape Colony was put out to tender and the Union Line succeeded in gaining the business, the first sailing taking place in September 1857.

For the next 15 years Union Line reigned supreme, despite the occasional ineffectual challenge, but in 1872 a formidable rival appeared in the shape of Donald Currie. Currie had left Cunard in 1862, after 20 years service, to found his own line of sailing ships trading from London to India. He was also interested in his brother's steam line trading from Leith to the Baltic and not much later formed his own Liverpool and Hamburg Line. In 1872, George Payne, who had set up the Cape and Natal Line in opposition to the Union Line, chartered two of Donald Currie's steamers for the service. Payne was in financial trouble, and while the ships were en route to South Africa he was obliged to tell Currie that he was unable to meet the cost of the charter and that Currie would have to bear the risks himself. At the urgent invitation of influential merchants and politicians at the Cape, disturbed by signs of complacency in the Union Line, Currie decided to stay, and sufficient financial inducement in the form of speed premiums was offered to him to remain in the trade until the forthcoming renewal of the Royal Mail contract in 1876, when he was offered a half share.

The following 24 years saw acute rivalry and a dramatic improvement as Union Line and Currie's Castle Mail Packets Company sought to outdo each other. Passage times were reduced from 23 to 17 days over this period and the size of mailships increased from 2,500 tons to 12,000 tons. Finally, late in 1899, talks between Sir Donald, as he now was, and his opposite in the Union Line Sir Francis Evans, led to the acquisition of the Union Line's assets and liabilities in March 1900 and the incorporation of the Union-Castle Line.

Sir Donald died in April 1909 and left a troubled legacy. For some years now difficulties had been caused by the adherence of the Union-Castle Line to the Rebate system, under which merchants shipping their goods exclusively by members of the South African Conference Lines were offered a Rebate. This was not to the liking of the Cape Colony Government, and had been the subject of a Royal Commission of which Owen Philipps had been a member. By 1911 impasse had been reached. The new South African Government had passed the Post Office Act under the terms of which no company operating the Rebate System could participate in the Royal Mail contract. The situation was closely watched by Philipps and also by Lord Pirrie, who was not unnaturally concerned at the prospect affecting the future of one of his best customers. Eventually, in April 1912, Royal Mail and Elder Dempster Lines jointly purchased the Ordinary Capital of Union-Castle for £5,173,572.50 and the Currie family retired. The cost of the investment was promptly rewarded by the declaration of a dividend which very substantially enabled the investors to recoup their outlay. Future prospects were assured by the signing of a new 10-year contract under the Post Office Act and preliminary plans were outlined for the construction of 6 new mailships by 1920. More immediate practical steps were taken to enhance the value of services by the offering of highly favourable freight rates on a wide range of South African agricultural produce, by the increase of refrigerated accommodation for South African fruit, and the carriage free of charge of pedigree breeding stock.

The First World War killed the ambitious mailship building programme before it had even begun, although two 19,000 ton steamers were completed in 1921 and 1922, a further pair ordered in 1916 having been cancelled in 1919 with no work done. A third steamer was ordered in 1923, but a few months later, apparently at the instigation of Harland and Wolff, the Union-Castle Directors agreed to fit diesel propulsion. In the course of the next few years 4 more motorships were built, 2 mailships and 2 inter-mediate liners.

At the time of the collapse of the Group in 1931, Union-Castle was in probably the most favourable position of all the Group members. Despite sizeable obligations in the form of repayments due under the Trade Facilities Acts, and £1 million due to White Star Line in respect of calls on capital issued, there was never any serious doubt that the company would survive. In consequence, the Voting Trustees for the Group were tacitly prepared to allow the new Union-Castle management to set their own course. The new Chairman was Robertson Gibb, an old Union Line man. Sir Vernon Thomson, Chairman of King Line and an erstwhile protege of Lord Kylsant, who had commenced his career in 1897 as the office boy, was Deputy Chairman of Union-Castle at the behest of the Preference Shareholders who, controlling the company by virtue of their dividend being in arrear, wished to be represented. Both these gentlemen proved thorns in the sides of the Voting Trustees, whose single major asset was the Union-Castle Ordinary Stock.

The liabilities were tackled with resolution. In 1932 Union-Castle alone among the Group companies discharged its liabilities to White Star Line, and sufficient progress was made in the discharge of other debts to enable the line to embark upon an ambitious programme of fleet building and modernisation that, on completion in 1939, cost £10 million and provided Union-Castle with the most modern fleet under the Red Ensign. There was no question as to the manner of propulsion of the new ships. Sir Vernon had first hand experience of the efficiency of the King Line motorships which had enabled that company to continue through the preceding 3 years, and experience with the 3 diesel powered mailships had been happier than that of the R.M.S.P. itself. These three were re-engined, 3 larger mailships were built, as well as 4 intermediate passenger liners, 6 fast fruit-carrying ships, a logical extension of Lord Kylsant's earliest policies, and a small feeder ship for the Southampton-Hamburg service.

Sir Vernon died early in 1953 and, after an indecisive interregnum, the Cayzer family's Clan Line offered to form a new company with Union-Castle. This was their third attempt, two earlier efforts having been rejected largely at Sir Vernon's behest, who had had his fill of Group involvement. This time the offer was to succeed, and in January 1956 Union-Castle and Clan Line became subsidiaries of British and Commonwealth Shipping Company Ltd.

The rundown of the Royal Mail service commenced in the 1960's when, for the first time, two cargo only mailships were built. Shortly after they entered service, two of the passenger mailships were transferred to Safmarine in 1966. Ten years later the combined effect of oil price increases and Jumbo jets saw the mail passenger liners start to go. Containerisation was scheduled for 1977, and in August and September of that year the last Union-Castle and Safmarine passenger sailings took place, the final Royal Mail sailing being that of SOUTHAMPTON CASTLE on 29th September 1977, 120 years and 17 days after the first. Today Union-Castle leases two modern refrigerated cargo ships, sailing under the Universal Freighters banner of Bermuda, on worldwide routes and not bearing Castle names.

CARNARVON CASTLE   *World Ship Photo Library*

LOCHKATRINE from an **R.M.S.P.** advertising card

T.M.S. "ADDA"

ELDER DEMPSTER LINES

A. S. Mallett Collection

ADDA from an Elder Dempster postcard

THE UNION-CASTLE Royal Mail Motorship "WARWICK CASTLE" (20,445 tons)

A. S. Mallett Collection

WARWICK CASTLE from a Union-Castle postcard

A NELSON LINER.

OROSENVINGE

FAST MAIL PASSENGER AND FREIGHT SERVICES TO SPAIN, PORTUGAL, CANARY ISLANDS, BRAZIL, URUGUAY, AND ARGENTINE.

A. S. *Mallett Collection*

A Highland class vessel from a Nelson Line postcard

UC1. CARNARVON CASTLE (1926-1962)

ON. 148766. 20063g. 12194n. 15790d. 630.7 x 73.5 x 41.5/32.8

4SCDA. 16 cyl: 33'' — 59''. 14000bhp. 2 screws. 16k.

Passengers: 311 First, 263 Second, 263 Third/Tourist as built
226 First, 254 Second, 188 Tourist in 1938
216 First, 401 Tourist in 1950

6.1926: Completed by Harland & Wolff Ltd., Belfast for Union-Castle Mail Steamship Company Ltd., and named CARNARVON CASTLE. 11.1937: Returned to builders for reconstruction completed 6.1938. Gross Tonnage now 20122, Net Tonnage 12989, Deadweight Tonnage 15524, Length BP 661.1/OA 686.3, powered by 2SCDA 20 cyl. $24\frac{7}{16}$'' — $55\frac{1}{8}$'' by builders 24000bhp. 20 knots. 9.1938: Completed the passage Nab Tower to Cape Town in 12 days 13 hours 38 minutes at 19.9 knots, a record. 8.9.1939: Requisitioned for service as an Armed Merchant Cruiser and converted at Simonstown armed with 8 6'' and 2 3'' A.A. guns. 9.10.1939: Commissioned. 5.12. 1940: While on patrol 700 miles NE Montevideo sighted auxiliary cruiser "Thor" and opened fire at 8.00 am, range 14000 yards. Action was broken off at 9.11 am when HMS CARNARVON CASTLE had fired 593 rounds and sustained 27 hits with 4 killed and 28 wounded. 7.12.1940: Arrived Montevideo and voyage repairs carried out using material removed from "Graf Spee". 11.1943: Released for service as troopship and converted at New York. 4.1947: Released to owners for service as Immigrant ship to South Africa. 4.1.1949: Arrived at Belfast for reconstruction and refitting for the Royal Mail Service. 15.6.1950: First post-war sailing in Royal Mail service. Gross Tonnage now 20141, Net Tonnage 11611, Deadweight Tonnage 14314. 1.6.1962: Laid up in Weymouth Bay and sold to Japanese shipbreakers. Arrived Mihara 8.9.1962, and delivered 12.9.1962.

LLANGIBBY CASTLE   *A. Duncan*

UC2. LLANGIBBY CASTLE (1929-1954)

ON. 161329. 11951g. 7199n. 8465d. 485.6 x 66.2 x 36.0/27.2

4SCSA 16 cyl: $29\frac{1}{8}$'' — $59\frac{1}{16}$''. 8500bhp. 2 scfews. 15k.

Passengers: 250 First, 200 Third/Tourist as built
212 First, 198 Tourist in 1947

1929: Completed by Harland & Wolff Ltd., Govan for Union-Castle Mail Steamship Company Ltd., and named LLANGIBBY CASTLE. 21/22.12.1940: Damaged by bombing at Liverpool. 16.1.1942: Torpedoed by U-402 in position 46.04N, 19.06W, with 1400 troops aboard. Stern gun and rudder were blown away. 17.1.1942: Attacked by enemy aircraft and drove it off, hitting it with anti-aircraft guns. 19.1.1942: Arrived Horta Bay. 2.2.1942: Left Horta Bay escorted by 3 Destroyers and a tug. 8.2.1942: Arrived Gibraltar. 6.4.1942: Left Gibraltar. 12.4.1942: Arrived in U.K. repaired and equipped as Infantry ship. 8.11.1942: Struck by 8'' shell which destroyed engineer's accommodation on boat deck, while landing troops at Oran. Returned fire and silenced battery with her 6'' gun. Subsequently collided with Dutch s.s. "Tegelberg" off Straits of Gibraltar resulting in severe damage. Troops were transferred to "Llanstephan Castle" for onward passage to Algiers. 3.1944: Re-equipped to cary 18 LCA's and 1 LCE, and at 5.30 am 6.6.1944 anchored off Courseulles and landed Canadian commandos, with the loss of 10 LCA's and 12 officers and men. 3.1945: Damaged in collision with s.s. "Antenor" off Calshot. 12.1946: Returned to owners, refitted by builders and delivered 9.7.1947. Gross Tonnage now 12039, Net Tonnage 7020. 18.6.1954: Completed last voyage. 29.6.1954: Left Tilbury and sold to John Cashmore Ltd., for demolition at Newport.

DUNBAR CASTLE. Note the open promenade deck forward *World Ship Photo Library*

UC3. DUNBAR CASTLE (1930-1940)

ON. 161420. 1002g. 5985n. 7780d. 471.2 x 61.2 x 29.6

4SCSA 12 cyl: $29\frac{1}{8}'' - 59\frac{1}{16}''$. 6200bhp. 2 screws. 14k.

Passengers: 200 First, 260 Third/Tourist

5.1930: Completed by Harland & Wolff Ltd., Govan for the Union-Castle Mail Steamship Company Ltd., and named DUNBAR CASTLE. 9.1.1940: Mined and sunk off Ramsgate in position 51.23N, 01.34E, with the loss of 6 lives. The wreck settled in shallow water with her back broken and upperworks and funnels plainly visible. 8.1949: Wreck "dispersed" by Royal Navy.

Note: DUNBAR CASTLE was readily distinguishable by her open verandah forward on the promenade deck. The other four motorships and subsequent Union-Castle liners had a glass enclosed promenade deck.

UC4. WINCHESTER CASTLE (1930-1960)

ON. 162489. 20109g. 12228n. 13005d. 631.6 x 75.5 x 37.5

4SCDA 16 cyl: 33'' — 63''. 14000bhp. 2 screws. 16k.

Passengers: 259 First, 243 Second, 254 Tourist/Third as built
189 First, 389 Tourist in 1949

8.1930: Completed by Harland & Wolff Ltd., Belfast for the Union-Castle Mail Steamship Company Ltd., and named WINCHESTER CASTLE. 25.8.1930: Attained 17.358 knots on trials. 16.2.1936: When homeward bound stranded on Chesil Bank, Portland Bill, but refloated next morning and docked pm at Southampton with damage of £20,000. 1938: Reconstructed and re-engined by builders. Gross Tonnage now 20012, Net Tonnage 12189 powered by 2SCDA 20 cyl: $24\frac{7}{16}'' - 55\frac{1}{8}''$, 24000bhp, 20 knots. 13.11.1948: Arrived at builders for refitting after war service as troopship and landing ship. 22.9.1949: First post-war voyage in Royal Mail Service. Gross Tonnage now 20001, Net Tonnage 11553, Deadweight Tonnage 12425. 9.1960: Sold to Nichimen Company Ltd. for £315,000 for demolition and arrived Mihara 5.11.1960.

WARWICK CASTLE. Compare her stern with the fuller version on ALCANTARA and CARNARVON CASTLE *World Ship Photo Library*

UC5. WARWICK CASTLE (1931-1942)

ON. 162527. 20445g. 12443n. 13667d. 651.5 x 75.5 x 37.4

4SCDA 16 cyl: 33" — 63". 14000bhp. 2 screws. 16k.

Passengers: 260 First, 245 Second, 254 Third/Tourist as built
262 First, 228 Second, 209 Tourist in 1938

1.1931: Completed by Harland & Wolff Ltd., Belfast for Union-Castle Mail Steamship Company Ltd., and named WARWICK CASTLE. 1938: Reconstructed and re-engined by builders, Gross Tonnage 20109, Net Tonnage 12240. Machinery 2 SCDA 20 cyl: $24\frac{7}{16}$" — $55\frac{1}{8}$". 24000bhp, speed 20 knots. 14.11.1942: Torpedoed and sunk by submarine U—413 whilst returning from the North African landings in position 39.16N, 13.25W with the loss of 63 lives.

WINCHESTER CASTLE *World Ship Photo Library*

HIGHLAND PATRIOT

NELSON LINE

Nelson Line was founded by the brothers Hugh and William Nelson to transport frozen meat from the Argentine to London, in 1890, and a fleet of 5 vessels bearing "Highland" names was soon acquired. Further additions to the fleet were made over the years, and in 1901 the company entered the passenger-carrying business. In 1910 a new fleet of 10 steamers was ordered. In 1913 the Line was acquired by the R.M.S.P. the company continuing to trade under its old colours.

In 1926 Nelson Line, with R.M.S.P. approval, ordered 5 new diesel-powered passenger-cargo liners, at 14000 tons almost twice the size of previous ships in the fleet, to counter 5 ships of similar size and speed ordered for the rival Vestey Group's Blue Star Line.

The new "Highland" motorships, which entered service in 1928-30, proved highly popular with passengers. Four served their original owners for 30 years — the fifth being wrecked early in her career and her identical replacement becoming a war loss. One of these four is now, 54 years on, the sole surviving Pirrie-Kylsant motorship.

The R.M.S.P. collapse led to the absorption of Nelson Line into the newly formed Royal Mail Lines in 1932.

FLEET LIST

N1. HIGHLAND MONARCH (1928-1960)

ON. 148158. 14137g. 8734n. 9070d. 523.4 x 69.4 x 37.1/28.1
4SCDA 16 cyl: 26¾' — 63''. 9500bhp. 2 screws. 15k.
Passengers: 135 First, 66 Interchangeable, 500 Third as built
              104 First, 335 Third in 1948
10.1928: Completed by Harland & Wolff Ltd., Belfast for Nelson Steam Navigation Company Ltd. and named HIGHLAND MONARCH. 4.8.1932: Fleet passed into ownership of Royal Mail Lines Ltd. 1948: Gross Tonnage now 14216, Net Tonnage 8536. 1960: Sold to W. H. Arnott Young & Company Ltd., for demolition at Dalmuir, and arrived 28.4.1960.

HIGHLAND MONARCH sailing on her maiden voyage *Furness Withy Group P.R. Dept.*

HIGHLAND CHIEFTAIN   *Skyfotos*

N2. HIGHLAND CHIEFTAIN (1929-1958)
ON. 148161. 14131g, 8730n, 9070d. 523.4 x 69.4 x 37.1/28.1

4SCDA 16 cyl: 26 " — 63". 9500bhp. 2 screws. 15k.
Passengers: 135 First, 66 Interchangeable, 500 Third as built
                       104 First, 335 Third in 1948

1.1929: Completed by Harland & Wolff Ltd., Belfast for Nelson Steam Navigation Company Ltd.,
and named HIGHLAND CHIEFTAIN. 4.8.1932: Fleet passed into ownership of Royal Mail Lines
Ltd. 11.10.1940: Damaged by bombs during air raid on Liverpool. 1948: Gross Tonnage now
14232, Net Tonnage 8666. 10.1958: Sold to Calpe Shipping Company Ltd., Gibraltar, and renamed
CALPEAN STAR. 1.1.1960: Sank in shallow water off Montevideo whilst in tow following an
engine room explosion and abandoned as a total loss.

HIGHLAND BRIGADE sailing on her maiden voyage   *Furness Withy Group P.R. Dept.*

HIGHLAND BRIGADE under tow after being mined off Singapore in January 1946
Furness Withy Group P.R. Dept.

N3. HIGHLAND BRIGADE (1929-1959)
ON. 148164. 14131g. 8732n. 9070d. 523.4 x 69.4 x 37.1/28.1
4SCDA 16 cyl: $26\frac{3}{4}''$ — 63''. 9500bhp. 2 screws. 15k.
Passengers: 135 First, 66 Interchangeable, 500 Third as built
          104 First, 335 Third in 1947
4.1929: Completed by Harland & Wolff Ltd., Belfast for Nelson Steam Navigation Company Ltd.,
and named HIGHLAND BRIGADE. 4.8.1932: Fleet passed into ownership of Royal Mail Lines
Ltd. 18.1.1946: Damaged by mine off Singapore. 11.1947: Re-opened London to River Plate
service. Gross Tonnage now 14216, Net Tonnage 8555. 1959: Sold to John S. Latsis, Piraeus
and renamed HENRIETTA. 1960: Renamed MARIANNA. 6.1965: Sold to Taiwan Shipbreakers
and broken up at Kaohsiung, arrived 29.6.1965.

N4. HIGHLAND HOPE (1930)
ON. 148170. 14129g. 8733n. 9070d. 523.4 x 69.4 x 37.1/28.1
4SCDA 16 cyl: $26\frac{3}{4}''$ — 63''. 9500bhp. 2 screws. 15k.
Passengers: 135 First, 66 Interchangeable, 500 Third
1.1930: Completed by Harland & Wolff Ltd., Govan for Nelson Steam Navigation Company
Ltd., and named HIGHLAND HOPE. 19.11.1930: Ran aground on NE Farihoes Rock, Portugal,
at 04.57 am in fog and abandoned as a total loss.

N5. HIGHLAND PRINCESS (1930-1959)
ON. 161859. 14128g. 8729n. 9070d. 523.4 x 69.4 x 37.1/28.1
4SCDA 16 cyl: $26\frac{3}{4}''$ — 63''. 9500bhp. 2 screws. 15k.
Passengers: 135 First, 66 Interchangeable, 500 Third as built
          102 First, 342 Third in 1947
2.1930: Completed by Harland & Wolff Ltd., Belfast for Nelson Steam Navigation Company
Ltd., and named HIGHLAND PRINCESS. 4.8.1932: Fleet passed into ownership of Royal Mail
Lines Ltd. 1948: Gross Tonnage now 14216, Net Tonnage 8536. 1959: Sold to John S. Latsis,
Piraeus and renamed MARIANNA. 1960: Sold to Czechoslovak Ocean Shipping, Czechoslovakia
and renamed SLAPY. 1960: Sold to People's Republic of China and renamed GUANG HUA,
registered in ownership of China Ocean Shipping Company. Still in Lloyds Register.

N6. HIGHLAND PATRIOT (1932-1940)
ON. 161883. 14157g. 8743n. 9070d. 523.4 x 69.4 x 37.1/28.1
4SCDA 16 cyl: $26\frac{3}{4}''$ — 63''. 9500bhp. 2 screws. 15k.
Passengers: 135 First, 66 Interchangeable, 500 Third
5.1932: Completed by Harland & Wolff Ltd., Belfast for Nelson Steam Navigation Company
Ltd., and named HIGHLAND PATRIOT. 4.8.1932: Fleet passed into ownership of Royal Mail
Lines Ltd. 1.10.1940: Torpedoed and sunk by submarine in position 52.20N, 19.04W whilst
on voyage Buenos Aires to the Clyde, with the loss of 3 lives.

KHETI

MOSS HUTCHINSON LINE

The Moss Hutchinson Line dates back to the first half of the nineteenth century when James Moss inaugurated a sailing ship service between Liverpool and the Mediterranean. The first steamships arrived in the 1840's and the company soon became heavily involved in the Egyptian cotton trade. Following the death of William Moss in 1873 the business was reorganised under the name Moss Steamship Co. Ltd. and was acquired by the Kylsant Group in 1916. Three years later J. & P. Hutchinson were also acquired by the Group as a subsidiary of the Moss Line. This concern had been formed in the mid 1850's and traded between Ireland, Scotland and France. During the Franco-Prussian War of 1870-71 Hutchinson's ships had carried medical supplies free of charge to the French army, and after the cessation of hostilities a grateful French Government permitted the company to adopt the French tricolour, with the Scottish thistle superimposed, as House flag.

Two motorships were built for Moss Line in 1927-9, and as occurred in other Group companies similar vessels were or had been built powered by the traditional steam engines for comparative purposes. This clearly points to a lack of centralised policy within the Group. The two motorships proved successful, as indeed may be claimed of all the cargo motorships not subject to rigid time schedules. In 1932 the Moss Line was restyled James Moss & Company (Moss Line) Ltd. and two years later the effective amalgamation with Hutchinsons was recognised with the formation of Moss Hutchinson Line on 6 April. Late in 1935 the company became a member of the large P & O Group when it was purchased by the General Steam Navigation Company Ltd.

Moss Hutchinson continued trading until 1978 when the last two ships were laid up. Although P & O had reorganised their shipping business into several large divisions within which the identity of the various lines was to be submerged in October 1971 for some reason this was not applied to Moss Hutchinson who continued to trade under their own colours.

FLEET LIST

MH1. KHETI (1927-1951)
ON. 149644. 2650g. 1323n. 330.7 x 47.3 x 19.4/20.7
4SCSA 8 cyl: $24\frac{13}{16}''-51\frac{3}{16}''$ by J. and G. Kincaid & Co. Ltd., Greenock. 1750bhp. 11k.
10.1927: Completed by Harland & Wolff Ltd., Greenock for Moss Steam Ship Co. Ltd. (J. Moss & Co., managers). 1930 Owners became James Moss & Co. (Moss Line) Ltd. 1934: Owners became Moss Hutchinson Line Ltd. 12.1940: Visted by H.M. King George VI during a tour of Liverpool docks. 1951: Sold to John Bruce & Co. Ltd., Glasgow (Mossgiel Steamship Co. Ltd., managers), and renamed ALCORA. 1958: Sold to Compania Maritima Mediterranee Limitada, San Jose, Costa Rica, Lebanese Flag and renamed GAY MED. 1964: Sold to Ibrahim Hassan Nahar, Lebanon and renamed MED STAR. 9.10.1967: Sank 30 miles S. of Pantellaria after springing a leak while on voyage Malta to Bayonne.

KUFRA   *Raul Maya Collection Montevideo*

MH2. KUFRA (1929-1940)
ON. 161126. 2608g. 1347n. 330.7 x 47.2 x 19.4
4SCSA 8 cyl: $24\frac{13}{16}''-51\frac{3}{16}''$ by J. G. Kincaid & Co. Ltd., Greenock. 1750bhp. 11k.
11.1929: Completed by Harland & Wolff Ltd., Glasgow for James Moss & Co. (Moss Line) Ltd. (J. Moss & Co., managers), and named KUFRA.1934: Owners became Moss Hutchinson Line Ltd. 24.6.1940: Lost by collision in position 44.11N, 02.00W while on voyage Verdonne Roads to Bayonne in ballast.

PINTO

MACANDREWS

To Robert MacAndrew and Company belongs the distinction of being the oldest established member of the Kylsant Group, for it was as early as 1770 that William MacAndrew despatched his first ship to the Iberian peninsula which was to be the mainstay of the company's services for 200 years. By the time of his death in 1819 the Line was well established in the fruit importing and shipping business although a family disagreement in 1853 saw a temporary parting of the ways between the shipping side in London and the fruit importing business in Liverpool. This did not outlast the retirement of the dissenting partner in 1871.

The management decided to sell to the Kylsant Group in 1917 largely as a result of the heavy losses suffered during the war and the cost of replacement. Accordingly the offer to purchase was accepted on 17 April and MacAndrew and Company Ltd. was registered to continue the trade. Two years later Mr. W. J. MacAndrew retired from the company he had joined in 1902 thus severing the family link. He lived long enough to see the line approach its Bi-centenary in 1970.

Two small engines aft motorships were built in 1922 for the line and five larger engines amidships successors followed in 1927, names all beginning with the letter 'P'. The basis of the design was carrying capacity of some 2000 tons on maximum draft of 17'6'' to trade from the smaller Spanish ports during the citrus season. At a later stage accommodation was fitted for up to 6 passengers.

United Baltic Corporation bought the company in 1935 and almost immediately ordered two improved versions of the 'P' class for the service. By this time a service to the Canaries in partnership with the Yeoward Line had started and attractive terms were offered to up to 12 passengers for the 17 day round voyage. During the war the 9 'P' motorships gave distinguished service in a variety of fields. Subsequently MacAndrews continued to trade until the late 1970's when the last ships were sold or transferred to the parent company.

FLEET LIST

A1. PINZON (1922-1951)
ON. 146218. 1365g. 634n, 2050d. 240.7 x 38.2 x 15.7/17.5
4SCSA 6 cyl: $24\frac{7}{16}$'' $- 38\frac{3}{8}$'', by builders. 1250bhp. 10k.
1.1922: Completed by Wm. Beardmore & Co. Ltd., Dalmuir for MacAndrews & Co. Ltd., and named PINZON. 1951: Sold to Rederi A/B Havnia, Mariehamm, Finland (Algot Johannson, manager), and renamed HAVNY. 2.1961: Sold to Scrapping S.A. Brussels for demolition.

PINZON   *World Ship Photo Library*

PIZARRO   *World Ship Photo Library*

A2. PIZARRO (1923-1941)
ON. 146688. 1367g. 637n. 2050d. 241.1 x 38.2 x 15.7/17.5
4SCSA 6 cyl: $24\frac{7}{16}''-38\frac{3}{8}''$ by builders. 1250bhp. 19k.
1.1923: Completed by Wm. Beardmore & Co. Ltd., Dalmuir for MacAndrews & Co. Ltd., and named PIZARRO. 31.1.1941: Torpedoed and sunk by submarine whilst in convoy 700 miles W. of Bishop Rock, position 49.03N, 19.40W with the loss of 23 lives.

PALACIO   *World Ship Photo Library*

A3. PALACIO (1927-1958)
ON. 149643. 1346g. 530n. 1950d. 270.1 x 39.1 x 15.6/17.1
4SCSA 6 cyl: $24\frac{13}{16}''-51\frac{3}{16}''$. 1500bhp. 11k.
10.1927: Completed by Harland & Wolff Ltd., Glasgow for MacAndrews & Co. Ltd., and named PALACIO. 1958: Sold to M. A. Bakhashab, Jeddah and renamed DAMMAM. 11.1965: Driven aground at Jeddah during heavy weather, subsequently refloated but broken up.

A4. PELAYO (1927-1942)

ON. 149650. 1346g. 530n. 1950d. 270.1 x 39.1 x 15.6/17.1
4SCSA 6 cyl: $24\frac{13}{16}''-51\frac{3}{16}''$. 1500bhp. 11k.

12.1927: Completed by Harland & Wolff Ltd., Glasgow for MacAndrews & Co. Ltd., and named PELAYO. 14.6.1942: Torpedoed and sunk by submarine while in convoy 400 miles W.N.W. Corunna position 43.18N, 17.38W with the loss of 16 lives.

PACHECO *World Ship Photo Library*

A5. PACHECO (1927-1958)

ON. 149654. 1346g. 530n. 1950d. 270.1 x 39.1 x 15.6/17.1
4SCSA 6 cyl: $24\frac{13}{16}''-51\frac{3}{16}''$. 1500bhp. 11k.

12.1927: Completed by Harland & Wolff Ltd., Glasgow for MacAndrews & Co. Ltd., and named PACHECO. 1958: Sold to M. A. Bakhashab, Jeddah and renamed ABQAIQ. 1961: Renamed STAR OF MECCA. 7.7.1962: Ran aground near Mukadda and became a total loss.

A6. PINTO (1928-1944)

ON. 149659. 1346g. 530n. 1950d. 270.1 x 39.1 x 15.6/17.1
4SCSA 6 cyl: $24\frac{13}{16}''-51\frac{3}{16}''$. 1500bhp. 11k.

2.1928: Completed by Harland & Wolff Ltd., Glasgow for MacAndrews & Co. Ltd., and named PINTO. 8.9.1944: Torpedoed and sunk by submarine off Tory Island in position 55.27N, 08.01W whilst acting as convoy rescue ship with the loss of 2 lives.

A7. PONZANO (1928-1939)

ON. 149664. 1346g. 530n. 1950d. 270.1 x 39.1 x 15.6/17.1
4SCSA 6 cyl: $24\frac{13}{16}''-51\frac{3}{16}''$. 1500bhp. 11k.

3.1928: Completed by Harland & Wolff Ltd., Glasgow for MacAndrews & Co. Ltd., and named PONZANO. 13.11.1939: Sunk after striking magnetic mine in the Thames Estuary position 51.29N, 01.25E.

GASCONY from a D. & C. MacIver postcard

MACIVER LINE

David MacIver and Company was established in 1875 by David MacIver formerly manager of the Cunard Line. After some years' trading to Mediterranean ports or on charter, a regular service from Liverpool to the River Plate was commenced in 1885, carrying cargo and a few first class passengers.

In 1919 the company was acquired by the R.M.S.P., and, in 1923 the first of three motorships was delivered.

Like Nelson Line, the MacIver Line was merged into the new Royal Mail Lines in 1932.

FLEET LIST

M1. ARABY (1923-1940)
ON. 147205. 4936g. 2944n. 7795d. 380.0 x 53.2 x 27.1/24.9
4SCSA 6 cyl: $29\frac{1}{8}''-59\frac{1}{16}''$. 1850bhp. 10½k.
3.1923: Completed by A. McMillan & Sons Ltd., Dumbarton for D. MacIver and Co. Ltd. and named ARABY. 4.8.1932: Fleet passed into ownership of Royal Mail Lines Ltd. 27.12.1940: Struck mine 9 cables west of Nore lightvessel and sank. 1949. Wreck dispersed.

M2. GASCONY (1925-1958)
ON. 147339. 4716g. 2631n. 7210d. 385.4 x 53.2 x 25.5/25.0
4SCSA 6 cyl: $29\frac{1}{8}''-59\frac{1}{16}''$. 1850bhp. 10½k.
11.1925: Completed by A. McMillan & Sons Ltd., Dumbarton for D. MacIver & Company Ltd. and named GASCONY. 4.8.1932: Fleet passed into ownership of Royal Mail Lines Ltd. 7.1958: Sold to Eckhardt & Company for demolition and arrived Hamburg 12.7.1958.

M3. BRITTANY (1928-1942)
ON. 149681. 4772g. 2849n. 400.4 x 55.2 x 25.7
4SCSA 8 cyl: $29\frac{1}{8}''-72\frac{3}{4}''$. 2500bhp. 12k.
1928: Completed by A. McMillan & Sons Ltd., Dumbarton for D. MacIver & Co. Ltd. and named BRITTANY. 4.8.1932: Fleet passed into ownership of Royal Mail Lines Ltd. 29.10.1942: Torpedoed and sunk by submarine in position 32.29N, 18.32W.

ARABY   *W. Lind Collection, Glasgow University Archives*

BRITTANY in Royal Mail Lines colours

A. Duncan

BRITTANY in her original colours

World Ship Photo Library

COMPANIES MANAGED BY DODD THOMSON AND COMPANY

This heading covers three tramp ship companies, viz

King Line Ltd. — founded 1889 — one third held by R.M.S.P.

Scottish Steamship Company Ltd. — founded 1896 — became a subsidiary of R.M.S.P. in 1919.

British Motorship Company Ltd. — founded 1925 as a subsidiary of R.M.S.P.

The first two companies were founded by Owen Philipps and until 1923 were managed by Philipps, Philipps and Company Ltd. King Line Ltd. itself was never a subsidiary of R.M.S.P.

Although Lord Kylsant was chairman and the directorate included his brother-in-law Delmer Davies-Evans and son-in-law future Earl of Coventry, day to day running of the fleet devolved upon the other two directors — George Dodd and Sir Vernon Thomson.

George Dodd had been a close friend of Lord Kylsant ever since their days as apprentices at Dent's in Newcastle. Dodd had briefly gone into partnership in Newcastle about the turn of the century, but this did not last and within a few years he moved to London and, probably at his friend's instigation, was appointed manager of the fleet of steamers building for John Philipps' Buenos Aires and Pacific Railway Company. By the end of 1918 that fleet had been either sunk or sold, and George Dodd had joined King Line Ltd.

Sir Vernon Thomson, the chartering director, joined Philipps, Philipps and Company Ltd. in 1897 as an office boy. By 1911 he was a director. Eight years later his services in the Ministry of Shipping had earned him his K.B.E. to add to his already high reputation in the tramp shipping world.

The acquisition of motorships by King Line was almost accidental. For some years unsuccessful efforts had been made to augment the fleet, until the breakthrough came in 1925.

The Canadian Government had for some years been considering the formation of its own steamship line in order to counter the liner conference system. Early in 1925 provisional agreement was reached with Sir William Petersen, of Newcastle, who travelled to Ottawa for detailed discussions. Meanwhile, two vessels of Monitor design were ordered from D. & W. Henderson & Company Ltd. at Glasgow.

On 12th June Sir William died, and shortly afterwards the Canadian Government announced the abandonment of its plans. Sir William's net estate, announced on 30th July, proved to be nil.

British Motorship Company Ltd. was incorporated on 6th August with issued capital of £50,000 for which modest sum the two vessels building at Henderson's were acquired, and in due course named KING JAMES and KING MALCOLM.

Distinctive vessels by any standards, they had three masts, with the unusual feature of two hatches (nos. 3 and 4) between the bridge house and engine room. They also boasted two parallel bulges, or corrugations, along the sides — on the theory that the concave shape between the bulges would channel water towards the propellor, thereby enhancing ecomony by improving speed. In practice this did not work out, and speed and fuel consumption did not differ appreciably from their conventionally hulled successors. Unfortunately, the bulges were prone to accidental damage and were also a source of structural weakness inasmuch as while the straight sided sections on the shelter deck space had the usual framing two feet apart, the corrugated section had framing five feet apart. This magnified stresses and conceivably led to KING JAMES' eventual loss.

In fairness it ought to be added that many admired these ships. One of KING JAMES' captains, A. J. MacInnes, recalled his pride in the ship in which he served both as Chief Officer and Captain, and in particular her unusual "all electric" auxiliaries.

The next nine ships emerged monthly from November 1927 — three flush deckers, four three-island vessels, and two three-island vessels with 'tween decks. Outstandingly economical, this fleet would regularly carry 7,500 tons of cargo at 10 knots on 7-8 tons oil per day — in 1928, and, those that survived, in 1958. Only four of the eleven survived the 1939-45 war — but their total service afloat aggregated 141 years, free of any major mechanical trouble. If little else is noted about these ships it is because their careers were unspectacular and notable only for their reliability.

These companies survived the collapse of the Group for three major reasons:-
Firstly: the building prógramme necessitated the sale of most of the R.M.S.P.

Harland and Wolff

KING EDGAR

debentures formerly held by King Line, leaving only £170,000 to be written off. This was within the company's resources.

Secondly: the new motorships could earn about £2,000 per voyage. This was sufficient to maintain their laid-up steam powered sisterships, and to service and repay their own building loans of £800,000.

Thirdly: Sir Vernon Thomson succeeded Lord Kylsant as chairman. Possibly Lord Kylsant would have preferred George Dodd to have taken over the reins of his 'first-born' — possibly George Dodd, too, would have preferred it — we do not know. All three men were strong, forceful characters, but Sir Vernon was the strongest. He was also the youngest, by 18 years, and these points may have tipped the scales in his favour. There is no evidence that he was on close personal, as distinct from professional, terms with either of his colleagues, in fact, he was by nature less than gregarious. His strength lay in sheer ability and determination to succeed — which was exactly what was required.

Sir Vernon also became Chairman of London Maritime Investment Company. It is likely that this concern was the vehicle used to acquire Scottish Steam Ship Company Ltd., and British Motorship Company Ltd., in 1933-4. The ramifications are not important — the latter was wound up in 1935 and its two ships transferred to the former concern, which was itself liquidated post-war after the sale of its last ship.

King Line became a subsidiary of Union-Castle Line in 1948, and is now part of the British and Commonwealth Group. The last conventional tramp was sold in 1973 and for ten years afterwards King Line operated a fleet of bulk carriers. Today it owns two products tankers, the only ships now owned by its Group.

KING MALCOLM   *World Ship Photo Library*

K1. KING JAMES (1925-1950)

ON. 148705. 5066g. 3129n. 9410d. 400.3 x 59.0 x 25.9
4SCSA oil engine. 6 cyl: $29\frac{1}{8}''$ — $59\frac{1}{16}''$. 1850bhp. 10k.

Ordered from D. & W. Henderson & Co. Ltd., Glasgow by Peterson & Co. London and launched
as RIVER OTTAWA. Sold to British Motorship Co. Ltd. 11.1925: completed as KING JAMES.
1935: Ownership transferred to the Scottish Steamship Co. Ltd. 1949: Laid up pending repairs.
1950: Sold to Constantin Arychides (Union Maritime & Shipping Co. Ltd., managers) Liberia
and renamed SOPHOCLYVE, 1954: Transferred to Compania Oceanica de Transportes SA (Union
Maritime & Shipping Co. Ltd., managers), Liberia 8.8.1960: Sank after springing a leak and being
abandoned in position 15.57N, 56.09E whilst on passage from Mormugao to Holland with a
cargo of ore.

SOPHOCLYVE formerly KING JAMES   *Skyfotos*

K2. KING MALCOLM (1925-1941)

ON. 148713. 5064g. 3128n. 9401d. 400.3 x 59.0 x 25.9
4SCSA oil engine 6 cyl: $29\frac{1}{8}''$ — $59\frac{1}{16}''$. 1850bhp. 10k.

Ordered from D. & W. Henderson & Co. Ltd., Glasgow by Petersen & Co., London and originally
to be named RIVER ST. LAWRENCE. Sold on the stocks to British Motorship Co. Ltd. 12.1925:
Completed as KING MALCOLM. 1935: Ownership transferred to the Scottish Steamship Co. Ltd.
31.10.1941: Torpedoed and sunk by U374 in position 47.40N 51.15W whilst on a voyage from
Haifa to Belfast and Garston via Table Bay and Sydney with a cargo of potash. There were no
survivors.

K3. KING EDGAR (1927-1945)

ON. 149947. 4536g. 2694n. 8211d. 400.6 x 54.8 x 23.6
4SCSA oil engine 6 cyl: $29\frac{1}{8}''$ — $59\frac{1}{16}''$.

11.1927: Completed by Harland & Wolff Ltd., Belfast for King Line Ltd. and named KING EDGAR.
2.3.1945: Torpedoed and sunk by U1302 in position 52.05N, 05.42W.

K4. KING EDWIN (1927-1943)

ON. 149964. 4536g. 2692n. 8211d. 400.6 x 54.8 x 23.6
4SCSA oil engine 6 cyl: $29\frac{1}{8}''$ — $59\frac{1}{16}''$. 1850bhp by the shipbuilders. 10k.

12.1927: Completed by Harland & Wolff Ltd., Belfast for King Line Ltd. and named KING EDWIN.
16.4.1943: Caught fire whilst unloading petrol and ammunition in Grand Harbour, Valetta, Malta
GC., and scuttled to avoid explosion. Declared a constructive total loss. 16.1.1944: Wreck struck
by SS EMPIRE TRAVELLER. 6.4.1945: Wreck raised and subsequently towed out to sea and
sunk.

KING EGBERT *World Ship Photo Library*

K5. KING EGBERT (1928-1939)
ON. 149979. 4535g. 2694n. 8211d. 400.6 x 54.8 x 23.6
4SCSA oil engine 6 cyl: $29\frac{1}{8}''-59\frac{1}{16}''$. 1850bhp. 10k.
1.1928: Completed by Harland & Wolff Ltd., Belfast for King Line Ltd. and named KING EGBERT.
12.11.1939: Mined and sunk 4 miles SW of Haisbro' Lightvessel, Norfolk.

KING JOHN at Vancouver *Captain G. F. Smith, O.B.E.*

K6. KING JOHN (1928-1940)
ON. 160356. 5228g. 3139n. 8330d. 400.7 x 54.8 x 27.2
4SCSA oil engine 6 cyl: $29\frac{1}{8}''-59\frac{1}{16}''$. 1850bhp. 10k.
2.1928: Completed by Harland & Wolff Ltd., Belfast for King Line Ltd. and named KING JOHN.
13.7.1940: Sunk by gunfire from the German raider WIDDER in a position 20N, 60W.

KING LUD *World Ship Photo Library*

K7. KING LUD (1928-1942)

ON. 160380. 5224g. 3136n. 8330d. 400.7 x 54.8 x 27.2
4SCSA oil engine 6 cyl: $29\frac{1}{8}''-59\frac{1}{16}''$. 1850bhp. 10k.
3.1928: Completed by Harland & Wolff Ltd., Belfast for King Line Ltd. and named KING LUD.
8.6.1942: Torpedoed and sunk by the Japanese submarine 1-10 in a position 20S, 40E approximately, whilst on a voyage from New York to Bombay via Table Bay, with a cargo of Government stores.

K8. KING NEPTUNE (1928-1957)

ON. 160404. 5224g. 3136n. 8330d. 400.7 x 54.8 x 27.2
4SCSA oil engine 6 cyl: $29\frac{1}{8}''-59\frac{1}{16}''$. 1850bhp. 10k.
4.1928: Completed by Harland & Wolff Ltd., Belfast for King Line Ltd. and named KING NEPTUNE. 21.3.1956: Ran ashore in heavy fog off Hottentot's Point, 30 miles north of Luderitz Bay while on passage in ballast from Lobito to Cape Town. 22.3.1956 refloated at 1.40 pm with aid of tug "Otto Siedle". 1957: Sold to Chip Hwa Shipping & Trading Co. Ltd., Singapore, and renamed WING ON. 1959: Transferred to Hong Kong registry. 1962: Sold to Hwa Aun (Hong Kong) Ltd. (Chip Hwa Shipping & Trading Co. Ltd., managers). 1963: Sold to Transportes Dorados SA Panama. 15.8.1968: Arrived at Kaohsiung to be broken up.

WING ON formerly KING NEPTUNE *World Ship Photo Library*

K9. KING ARTHUR (1928-1942)

ON. 160458. 5228g. 3139n. 8330d. 400.7 x 54.8 x 27.2
4SCSA oil engine 6 cyl: $29\frac{1}{8}''-59\frac{1}{16}''$. 1850bhp. 10k.
5.1928: Completed by Harland & Wolff Ltd., Belfast for King Line Ltd. and named KING ARTHUR.
15.11.1942: Torpedoed and sunk by U67 in a position 10.30N, 59.50W.

KING STEPHEN   *World Ship Photo Library*

K10. KING STEPHEN (1928-1957)

ON. 160496. 5274g. 3171n. 8330d. 400.7 x 54.8 x 27.2
4SCSA oil engine 6 cyl: $29\frac{1}{8}''-59\frac{1}{16}''$. 1850bhp. 10k.
6.1928: Completed by Harland & Wolff Ltd., Belfast for King Line Ltd. and named KING STEPHEN. 1957: Sold to Vanguard Shipping Co. Ltd. (World-Wide Shipping Co. Ltd., managers), Hong Kong and renamed GOLDEN DELTA. 1962: Sold to The Corinthian Shipping Co. Ltd. (World-Wide Shipping Co. Ltd., managers), Hong Kong. 1956: Sold to Fuji Marden & Co. Ltd., who commenced demolition at Hong Kong 4.3.1965.

K11. KING WILLIAM (1928-1959)

ON. 160516. 5274g. 3171n. 8330d. 400.7 x 54.8 x 27.2
4SCSA oil engine 6 cyl: $29\frac{1}{8}''-59\frac{1}{16}''$. 1850bhp. 10k.
7.1928: Completed by Harland & Wolff Ltd., Belfast for King Line Ltd. and named KING WILLIAM. 7.1959: Sold to Hanwa Co. Ltd., Tokyo for breaking up.

KING WILLIAM   *A. Duncan*

BRITANNIC

WHITE STAR LINE

The purchase of White Star Line from American interests late in 1926 was intended to be the crowning triumph of Lord Kylsant's life. Unfortunately, it turned out to be a major contributing factor to the collapse of the Group.

There were two White Star Lines. The first, founded in 1852 by John Pilkington and Henry T. Wilson, operated sailing vessels to Australia, expanding into steam in 1863. Four years later a financial crisis resulted in the collapse of Royal Bank of Liverpool, the line's bankers, leaving White Star Line owing £527,000.

The name, flag and goodwill were bought for £1,000 by T. H. Ismay, who registered Oceanic Steam Navigation Company Ltd. on 6th September, 1869, and built a fleet of steamers for the North Atlantic route. Meanwhile, the link with Australia was maintained by Ismay's fleet of sailing ships.

Surplus tonnage in the mid-1870's led to arrangements with the American Occidental and Oriental Steamship Company to charter a number of White Star liners for trans-Pacific services — a connection that lasted until 1906. White Star Line re-entered the Australian trade in 1899, seventeen years after entering the New Zealand trade in partnership with Shaw, Savill and Albion.

The early years of the twentieth century saw dramatic changes. T. H. Ismay had died late in 1899, and was succeeded by his son J. Bruce Ismay. In 1902 the American International Mercantile Marine, headed by J. P. Morgan and supported by Lord Pirrie, offered £10 million for the ordinary share capital. It was an offer the 75 shareholders could scarcely be expected to refuse, and, despite considerable regrets among the Ismay family, the offer was accepted.

For thirty years White Star had been regular customers of Harland & Wolff, and Lord Pirrie clearly saw the realisation of his dream of building a 1,000 ft. liner moving perceptibly closer. For the time being, however, 850 ft. would have to suffice — and three were ordered, only one of which was ever to complete a commercial voyage.

By the middle 1920's White Star was established as the joint 'senior partner' on the North Atlantic, equal to Cunard, but by now the Morgan Combine were anxious to sell. Eventually, and after several unsuccessful bids from other sources, the R.M.S.P. agreed to pay £7 million to purchase the company on 1st January 1927. Ten days later, a new company, White Star Line Ltd., was formed with £9 million capital — £5 million in Preference Shares issued to the public, and the balance in Ordinary Shares issued on a partly paid basis to other group companies.

At this time the R.M.S.P. Group finances were already under pressure and time was to prove that the White Star purchase was the proverbial 'last straw'. Frank Bustard, sometime passenger manager of White Star wrote:-

"Many leading ship owners in the past have regarded an entry into the highly competitive North Atlantic passenger trade as a fitting climax to a shipping career and Kylsant was no exception to this ambition. After the first World War Kylsant started his own R.M.S.P. service to New York, operating from Hamburg and Southampton with four ships transferred from the South American trade. The service was not a success, but Kylsant's appetite for the North Atlantic trade was whetted."

By 1924 Kylsant had gained control of the great ship-building concern of Harland & Wolff Ltd. through shareholdings in various concerns under his control.

On Viscount Pirrie's death in 1924, Lord Kylsant took over the chairmanship of Harland & Wolff. It does not require much imagination to realise the attraction Kylsant felt for next acquiring the White Star Line from American ownership, so consolidating his shaky R.M.S.P. position in the New York trade and, most important of all, realising Harland & Wolff's dream of a 1,000 ft. liner.

Kylsant acquired the White Star Line (Oceanic Steam Navigation Company Ltd.) from I.M.M. for £7,000,000 (an extravagant figure) on 1st January, 1927 and became Hon. President and Joint Managing Director, with Mr. Harold Sanderson as Chairman and Joint Managing Director. A company was then formed by Kylsant, known as White Star Line Ltd. to hold the shares of the O.S.N. Company, with himself as Chairman of the W.S.L. Ltd., and Mr. Sanderson as Deputy Chairman.

Immediately O.S.N. was required to pay its new holding company dividends which should have been ploughed back into the concern in those difficult years, as for instance:-

1927   —   Dividend of £450,000

1928   —   Dividend of £400,000 — with a Bank overdraft of £337,839

1929   —   Dividend of £400,000 — with a Bank overdraft of £896,844
(Mr. Harold A. Sanderson relinquished his seat on the Board)

1930   —   Dividend . . . NIL . . . with a Bank overdraft of £1,239,382.

For the first time in its history of 61 years the White Star Line operated at a loss — namely, £379,069.

Throughout this time certain fundamental miscalculations in management were made:-

a. The representation of the company in America, including all booking arrangements for passengers and freight and all terminal facilities were left in the hands of Mr. P. A. S. Franklin (I.M.M. Co.). This was a grievous mistake in view of Mr. Franklin's growing interest in the operation of American-flag tonnage, and it left the White Star Line at a serious disadvantage compared with Cunard and all other North Atlantic lines enjoying their own 100% representation in America.

b. The forced removal in July 1929 of the company's long established Head Office and staff from Liverpool to the Kylsant Headquarters at Royal Mail House, Leadenhall Street, London, was a psychological blunder and a heavy expense to the White Star Line.

c. Transfer to the W.S.L. (Canadian Service) of the R.M.S.P. Company OHIO and ORCA (renamed ALBERTIC and CALGARIC) — two most unsuitable vessels for the trade.

The situation deteriorated further during the next three years with White Star showing losses of

— £450,777 in 1931

— £152,045 in 1932

— £353,552 in 1933

In 1934 White Star Line was merged with Cunard, as part of the arrangements for financing the ships that were to become the 'Queens'. The Government, and Neville Chamberlain in particular, had decided that there was not room for two express British services, and White Star Line's considerable deficit — only Union-Castle of all Group companies ever honoured the calls on part-paid capital issued to them (to the tune of £1 million) — coupled with the 1928 acquisition of the Commonwealth Line from the Australian Government, which ultimately cost them £1.9 million and gave nothing to show for it when the Australians called in the mortgages and sold the fleet to Shaw Savill.

Under these circumstances the White Star contribution to motorship development was limited — but if quantity was lacking, quality was there in plenty. BRITANNIC and GEORGIC were the largest of the Kylsant motorships, and their 10-cylinder engines were the most powerful installed. The press waxed lyrical — "The engine room is so cool that electric radiators are used to keep it warm in winter." (Daily Mail) — "So small is the vibration." (Daily Dispatch) — and the memorable claim that BRITANNIC could move "one ton one mile on a thimbleful of oil". At the time of their completion further ships of the type were predicted — but financial reasons ordained otherwise, and similarly the 1,000 ft. OCEANIC, ordered on 18th June, 1928 and laid down ten days later, never progressed further.

BRITANNIC was the last survivor from White Star Line, whose colours she wore until the end of 1960 when she docked at the breakers' yard at Inverkeithing.

Skyfotos

GEORGIC postwar

W1. BRITANNIC (1930-1960)

ON. 162316. 26943g, 16445n, 14070d. 683.6 x 82.4 x 48.6/34.2

4SCDA 20 cyl: 33 '' — 63''. 17000bhp. 2 screws. 18¼k.

Passengers: 504 Cabin, 551 Tourist, 498 Third as built

               469 First, 564 Tourist in 1948

6.1930: Completed by Harland & Wolff Ltd., Belfast for White Star Line Ltd., and named BRITANNIC, commencing maiden voyage Liverpool — New York on 28.6.1930. 10.5.1935: Owners became Cunard White Star Line Ltd. 1947-8: Reconditioned after war-time service as troopship, Gross Tonnage now 27778, Net Tonnage 15811. 5.1948: First post-war commercial voyage Liverpool — New York. 12.1960: Sold to British Iron & Steel Company Ltd. for demolition and arrived Inverkeithing 19.12.1960.

GEORGIC *F. W. Hawks*

W2. GEORGIC (1932-1943)

ON. 162365. 27759g. 16839n. 14500d. 683.6 x 82.4 x 48.6/35.0

4SCDA 20 cyl: 33 '' — 63''. 17000bhp. 2 screws. 18¼k.

Passengers: 479 Cabin, 557 Tourist, 506 Third

6.1932: Completed by Harland & Wolff Ltd., Belfast for White Star Line Ltd., and named GEORGIC, commencing maiden voyage Liverpool — New York on 25.6.1932. 10.5.1935: Owners became Cunard White Star Line Ltd. 14.7.1941: Bombed and burnt out by enemy aircraft at Port Tewfik, Suez Canal. Towed to Bombay for emergency repairs and 3.1943 arrived Belfast for permanent repairs and refitting as troopship. Sold to H.M. Government. 16.12.1944: Re-entered service, Gross Tonnage now 27469, Net Tonnage 15463. 1.1956: Sold to shipbreaking Industries Ltd., Faslane and arrived 1.2.1956.

SHAW SAVILL AND ALBION

Shaw Savill and Albion origins are traceable to the 1830's, when two of four Henderson brothers, Patrick (Paddy) and George, founded the Albion Line at Glasgow. This line of sailing ships entered the New Zealand trade in 1855, and three years later were challenged by Shaw, Savill and Company.

The founders of the Albion Line were interesting. The other two brothers founded the shipbuilding firm of D. & W. Henderson — which eventually became a subsidiary of Harland & Wolff. Two of the four brothers were associated in forming the Anchor Line, while the family Henderson Line operated on the Burma route for over a century.

1882 proved notable in two ways. It saw the amalgamation of Shaw, Savill and Company with the Albion Line in November. It also saw, as every English housewife must have learnt from the posters displayed at her local butcher's shop, the arrival of the first cargo of New Zealand mutton and lamb in England — 130 tons, or 4,460 sheep, 449 lambs and 22 pigs — aboard the ship DUNEDIN.

At the same time the first steamers were being built for the route to fulfil the terms of a government mail contract, necessitating five steamers, three of which were owned and manned by the White Star Line, which began acquiring shares in Shaw Savill and Albion a few years later, and which by 1926 totalled 44% of the issued capital.

The incorporation of White Star Line into the International Mercantile Marine in the opening years of the twentieth century was not to affect Shaw Savill unduly, more important was the acquisition of a strong link and shareholding in George Thompson's rival Aberdeen Line, and, in July 1910, an initial acquisition, subsequently increased, of slightly over 25% of Shaw Savill's issued capital by Sir John Ellerman.

Shaw Savill fell into the R.M.S.P. Group after the purchase of White Star Line in 1927, and the subsequent purchase (for £994,000) of Sir John Ellerman's majority holding. These purchases had already strained the Group's finances, but worse was to follow. In May 1928 £1,850,000 was paid for the Australian Government's Commonwealth Line. This might have proved successful — the seven ships had cost £7 million only six years previously — and the conference rights were worthwhile — but the Group had not the funds and White Star, in whose name the contract deed was completed, were themselves in difficulties.

After the collapse, Shaw Savill were acquired by Furness Withy — negotiations being completed in 1936.

The company planned to build two 20,000-ton, 17 knot, passenger-cargo vessels in 1926, possibly to counter the rival New Zealand Company's "Rangi" class, but these never materialised, and until 1939 Shaw Savill's passenger fleet consisted of ex-Aberdeen liners and their own pre-1914 veterans. Instead, four twin-screw, refrigerated motorships were ordered, with Sulzer engines and completed in 1928. Three survived thirty years and, in April 1933, two derivatives were built at Belfast with nine more following up to 1945, all proving notable for their performance and exacting wartime service.

The new Shaw Savill passenger-cargo liner eventually appeared in 1939 — the 27,000-ton DOMINION MONARCH, catering for 508 first class passengers in considerable luxury and over 10,000 tons cargo, mainly refrigerated. She was powered by four Doxford opposed-piston engines, each driving its own propellor, at a speed of 19 knots and, with Union-Castle's CAPETOWN CASTLE, was the largest ship on the Empire routes (excluding Canada) pre-war.

FLEET LIST

S1. ZEALANDIC (1928-1941)
ON. 149300. 8281g, 5109n, 10390d. 482.6 x 64.2 x 30.8/28.7
2SCSA 12 cyl: 31'' — 43'' by Wallsend Slipway and Engineering Company Ltd. 7500bhp. 2 screws. 14k.
3.1928: Completed by Swan Hunter and Wigham Richardson Ltd., Wallsend for Shaw Savill and Albion Company Ltd., and named ZEALANDIC. 16.1.1941: Torpedoed and sunk by submarine 450 miles south of Vestmann Islands in position 58.28N, 20.43W while on passage Liverpool to Australia, with the loss of 74 lives.

A. Duncan

KARAMEA

ZEALANDIC   *A. Duncan*

TARANAKI   *Furness Withy Group P.R. Dept.*

S2. TARANAKI (1928-1963)
ON. 149304. 8286g, 5054n, 10460d. 483.0 x 64.2 x 30.8/28.8
2SCSA 12 cyl: 31″ — 43″ by builders. 7500bhp. 2 screws. 14k.
5.1928: Completed by Fairfield Shipbuilding and Engineering Company Ltd., Glasgow for Shaw Savill and Albion Company Ltd., and named TARANAKI. 1963: Sold to Japanese shipbreakers and arrived Aioi 11.9.1963.

COPTIC in wartime rig

S3. COPTIC (1928-1965)

ON. 149312. 8281g, 5111n, 10390d. 482.6 x 64.2 x 30.8/28.7
2SCSA 12 cyl: 31'' — 43'' by Wallsend Slipway and Engineering Company Limited.
7500bhp. 2 screws. 14k.
7.1928: Completed by Swan Hunter and Wigham Richardson Ltd., Wallsend for Shaw Savill and Albion Company Ltd.,and named COPTIC. 1965: Sold to Belgian shipbreakers and arrived Antwerp 14.7.1965.

S4. KARAMEA (1928-1960)

ON. 149326. 8281g, 5052n, 10460d. 483.0 x 64.2 x 30.8/28.7
2SCSA 12 cyl: 31'' — 43'' by builders. 7500bhp. 2 screws. 14k.
8. 1928: Completed by Fairfield Shipbuilding and Engineering Company Ltd., Glasgow for Shaw Savill and Albion Company Ltd., and named KARAMEA. 2.1941: Attacked and bombed by enemy aircraft and hit by one bomb which failed to explode. Subsequently refitted and refrigerated capacity increased, time out of service totalling 321 days. 1960: Sold to British Iron and Steel Corporation and arrived T. W. Ward Ltd., Inverkeithing 8.12.1960.

ZEALANDIC

FLEET LISTS PART TWO

Chronology of the 25 inshore and river motorships operated by member companies of the Kylsant Group.

1. Details are extracted from Lloyds Registers.
2. Ships are listed in order of acquisition by their owners. In all cases the dates following the name are those of entering and leaving the fleet.
3. On the first line is given the ship's Official Number (ON) in the British registry followed by her tonnages gross ('g') nett ('n') and deadweight ('d'), and her dimensions. Deadweight tonnages are approximate. Minor variations in tonnage measurements during a ship's career have been ignored. Dimensions are the registered dimensions — length between perpendiculars x breadth x moulded depth — in feet and tenths of a foot. Where available alternative details given are length overall and loaded draught. All measurements have been expressed in Imperial measures. Engine details given include number and size of cylinders, working particulars and brake horse-power.
4. A number of the vessels built for the Argentine Navigation Company Ltd. still appear in Lloyds Register up to February 1984. Certain others have been deleted on the grounds that they are only operational on rivers. Owing to present complications in communication between the United Kingdom and Argentina it cannot authoritatively be stated that all the vessels shown in this list as being in existence are in fact so.

BRITISH COASTAL SERVICES

For the first half of the twentieth century Liverpool was a world port. With an industrial hinterland stretching eastwards to the Pennines it was the centre of tobacco, corn and cotton trading, and an administrative centre for a sizeable amount of British shipping. As recently as 1958 its Ship Owners Association had sixty-seven members who 'entered' 4.6M: gross tons of shipping. Although a port disadvantaged by an unfavourable natural setting — a tidal estuary with a major silting problem — it faces Ireland and attracted much transit trade.

Behind the glamour of the deepsea trades, Liverpool spawned a mass of coastal ship operators. These ranged from one man owner-masters to splendid reproductions, in miniature, of the trans-Atlantic passenger and mail carrying liners. The network for the carriage of coastal cargoes had their only serious competition from the railways. So economic was the carriage of cargo by sea that when the Manchester Ship Canal opened in 1894 the Powell Line started a cargo service — carrying as much as 1,200 tons at a time between Liverpool and Manchester.

In the worst summer for ship losses in World War One, 1917, the Group bought the leading Liverpool coasting company, which had been formed in 1913 by the amalgamation of Powell Line (formed 1850), Hough Line (1852 and long, friendly rivals of the Crams who ran Powell) and Bacon Line (1850) and now traded under the collective title of Coast Lines. Thereafter acquisitions by the newly styled and titled group came thick and fast. It was a period of change in the make up of British shipping. Dissipated by a catastrophic war after a century of peace, family companies faced problems compounded by heirs killed or maimed on the western front; ships being torpedoed in sight of shore; unprecedented official bureaucracy, and even tax being claimed; inflation, labour problems and disrupted trading patterns. Amongst those who sold out to the Group were Stocks, Turnbull in 1918 with three ships; a year later the Royal Line (M. Langlands and Sons Limited), who dated back to the 1820's and who had a colourful history operating a Liverpool-Glasgow passenger service that had grown into a premier service on the Scottish coast; and, the Volana Shipping Company (incorporated 1888) which gave Coast Lines a Liverpool-Cardiff-Buryport route.

The buying spree of companies went on into 1920 with the Little Western Steamship Company who had built up a Bristol to London service with calls at Newport, Penzance, Plymouth and Tor Bay ports. In 1923 Coast Lines absorbed the Gralmainston Shipping Company Limited of Glasgow who operated services out of the Clyde to Ulster. The

INNISFALLEN

wealth of South Wales underpinned by coal had produced the London, Welsh Steamship Company in 1908 which was bought out in 1924. But interest in Ireland persisted with Dundalk and Newry being added in 1926, and Michael Murphy Limited also in 1926.

The prime operators between England, Scotland and Ireland were British and Irish Steam Packet who had been bought in 1917 at the same time as Powell, Bacon, and Hough Lines, and had thus been operated by Coast Lines from its start. Whilst B & I were centred on Dublin as their terminal port, the acquisition, all in 1919, of Laird Line, Belfast Steamship, City of Dublin Steam Packet and, in 1920 Burns Steamship, ensured that this was not only reinforced but also extended to dominate the trades in and out of Belfast as well.

But the jewel in the Coast Lines collection was the addition in 1928 of David MacBrayne Limited who were the link to the west Highlands and their Islands; the L.M.S. retained a shareholding in the Company.

What strategic value did Coast Lines contrinute to the Group? It made good sense to ensure that Harland and Wolff received its raw materials in ships that the Group controlled and it added some price stability to the yard's products. In the era before road transport a significant amount of import and export cargo was fed to, and taken from, the ocean going ships by coasters; they enabled through bills of lading to be given between ports which have long been forgotten as such — cattle food from Opobo (Nigeria) to Bridgewater and grain from the River Plate to a flour mill on the Medway. There was also the transport of coal which, although the Group looked forward to the new energy, oil, played a dominant part in the U.K. trade.

Except for putting a famous trio of motorships on the services between Liverpool and Belfast, Coast Lines was left out of the Group's switch to diesel engine tonnage. There was in the 1920's a big development gap between truck engines and big medium speed ship's engines and no real concurrent development of high (or otherwise) speed engines for small ships. Steamships were built throughout the period but it was not until 1935-1940 that Coast Lines really became serious about motorships.

BELFAST STEAMSHIP COMPANY LIMITED

The Kylsant-Pirrie axis between London and Belfast made the ownership of the principal sealink a necessity and was probably the main motivation for the acquisition of Coast Lines in 1917, although Belfast Steamship came into the Group, finally, in 1919.

When the ULSTER MONARCH came into service in 1929 she was the world's first cross-channel diesel engined ship. The Belfast company had been synonymous with progressive ships ever since it had merged with its Liverpool rivals, Langtrys, in 1859. Despite periods of acute competition (both company's forebears had, in 1928, reduced the steerage class fare to 3d — which included a meal — to hold their market share) the company built the most modern ships possible. The DYNAMIC of 1883 although with a GRT of only 884 had features that Thomas Ismay was building into his transatlantic White Star ships. These included electric light and bilge keels to reduce rolling. Thus the Kylsant trio maintained a pioneering tradition as well as the nightly sailing in each direction. It is interesting to recall that alhtough the ships in the passenger cargo services did, from 1886 onwards, sail from Belfast at a uniform hour, Liverpool had a problem with the sand bar at the mouth of the Mersey and any regular service was until 1 October 1893, dependent on high tides. Spurred on by competition from the new Manchester Ship Canal, the Mersey Docks and Harbour Board, employing two hopper dredgers, widened the channel and dug out the depth to twenty-five feet at low tide. This work was preserved by the scouring work encouraged by revetment walls.

Competing with L.M.S.'s own Heysham-Belfast route, Belfast Steamship also carried cargo to Larne and Londonderry in small coasters of which never less than a dozen were in service.

The ULSTER MONARCH's operational success was such that the design was used as a template for successive Coast Lines group-wide passenger cargo ships that needed a high proportion of cabin accommodation and the main features that were inked into plans in Belfast in 1925 can be identified through a series of ships up to the ULSTER QUEEN and ULSTER PRINCE built in 1967.

97

BRITISH AND IRISH STEAM PACKET COMPANY and CITY OF CORK S.P. COMPANY

With all of Ireland part of the U.K. at the turn of the century there had always been a large amount of regular trans-Irish sea traffic. Ireland needed coal and manufactured goods, and England needed labour and livestock. At the regardless-of-cost end of the trade was the carriage of mails which, in the 1880's was as well organised and just as fast as it is in the 1980's. To carry mail and passengers, complementing the railways, there were never fewer than three main Irish Sea companies. The most consistent and usually successful of these was British and Irish. Although after being established in 1836 the company concentrated on the Dublin to London direct route, the advent of nationwide railway networks and competition from Waterford put them into opening a Dublin-Liverpool service in 1848 and there they have been ever since.

The City of Cork Company had irself arisen from a split of two companies — one into deep sea trading and the other into coastal routes — in 1871. It still had a separate entity operating between the Mersey and Cork when the multimarriage within Coast Lines, and the R.M.S.P. Group, occurred in 1917.

ULSTER MONARCH   *A. Duncan*

FLEET LIST

I1. ULSTER MONARCH (1929-1966)
ON. 148163. 3735g. 1769n. 920d. 346.0 x 46.2 x 15.2/14.9
4SCSA 20 cyl: $24\frac{13}{16}''-38\frac{9}{16}''$. 5000bhp. 2 screws. 18k.
6.1929: Completed by Harland & Wolff Ltd., Belfast for Belfast Steamship Co. Ltd. and named ULSTER MONARCH. 1946: Refitted by builders following wartime service. Gross tonnage now 3851. 12.1966: Sold to Van Heyghen Freres for breaking up at Ghent and arrived 8.12.1966.

I2. ULSTER QUEEN (1930-1940)
ON. 161857. 3735g. 1769n. 920d. 346.0 x 46.2 x 15.2/14.9
4SCSA 20 cyl: $24\frac{13}{16}''-38\frac{9}{16}''$. 5000bhp. 2 screws. 18k.
2.1930: Completed by Harland & Wolff Ltd., Belfast for Belfast Steamship Co. Ltd., and named ULSTER QUEEN. 2.1940: Ran aground in Ramsey Bay, Isle of Man but refloated 25.3.1940 and sold to H.M. Government. Fitted out for service as Anti-Aircraft Ship. 1943: Converted for use as Fighter Direction Ship. 1945: Laid up at Milford Haven after the war and struck off the Navy List in 4.1946. 1951: Sold to breaking up in Belgium.

ULSTER QUEEN　　　　　　　　　　　　　　　*World Ship Photo Library*

ULSTER QUEEN as a radar ship　　　　　　　*World Ship Photo Library*

13. ULSTER PRINCE (1930-1941)
ON. 161858. 3735g. 1769n. 920d. 346.0 x 46.2 x 15.2/14.9
4SCSA 20 cyl: $24\frac{13}{16}''-38\frac{9}{16}''$. 5000bhp. 2 screws. 18k.
3.1930: Completed by Harland & Wolff Ltd., Belfast for Belfast Steamship Co. Ltd., and named
ULSTER PRINCE. 4.1941: Ran aground near Nauplia, Greece, bombed and became total loss.

14. INNISFALLEN (1930-1940)
ON. 152222. 3019g. 1334n. 800d. 321.0 x 45.7 x 15.2/14.8
4SCSA 20 cyl: $24\frac{13}{16}''-39\frac{9}{16}''$. 5000bhp. 2 screws. 18k.
6.1930: Completed by Harland & Wolff Ltd., Belfast for City of Cork Steam Packet Co. Ltd.,
and named INNISFALLEN. 21.12.1940: Mined and sunk at entrance to Canada Dock, Liverpool.

DAVID MACBRAYNE LTD.

David MacBrayne entered the shipping business in Feburary 1851 as a partner in David Hutchenson & Company, trading in the West Highlands and Islands of Scotland. The concern continued trading in David MacBrayne's name, following the retirement of the two Hutchenson brothers, in 1879, the business being formed into a limited company in 1905, and acquired by the R.M.S.P. Group in 1928.

The contract terms governing the West Highlands trade necessitated the immediate construction of four passenger vessels, of which one (LOCHNESS) was steam powered. Additionally, one cargo only vessel, LOCHSHIEL, was built.

Prior to the acquisition of the company by the R.M.S.P. Group one vessel built in 1908, LOCHMOR, was powered by paraffin motors by L. Gardner and Sons. Her new colleague LOCHFYNE was equally advanced, her diesel-electric machinery attracting a great deal of interest.

FLEET LIST

H1. LOCHSHIEL (1929-1951)
ON. 160274. 208g. 102n. 105.8 x 26.1 x 8.5/9.0
2SCSA 6 cyl: $12\frac{1}{2}''$ - 15'' by L. Gardner and Son Ltd., Manchester. 300bhp. $9\frac{1}{2}$k.

1929: Completed by H. Robb Ltd., Leith for David MacBrayne (1928) Ltd. and named LOCHSHIEL. 1951: Sold to O. Ferris, Glasgow (H. J. A. Ryeland, manager) and renamed EUGENE 7.1955: Broken up in Belgium.

H2. LOCHEARN (1930-1964)
ON. 161916. 542g. 206n. 155.7 x 29.1 x 9.0
2SCSA 12 cyl: $12\frac{1}{2}''$ — 15'' by L. Gardner and Son Ltd. Manchester. 600bhp. 2 screws; $9\frac{1}{2}$k.

1930: Completed by Ardrossan Dockyard Co. Ltd., Ardrossan for David MacBrayne (1928) Ltd. and named LOCHEARN. 1948-49: Re-engined with 12 cyl. Paxman Ricardo diesels speed now 11 knots 8.1964: Sold to Tamis SA Panama and renamed NAIAS. 1966: Sold to J. Katsoulakos, Panama, name unchanged and converted to a yacht. 1970: Sold to Naiaskazi Compania Maritima S.A., Panama name unchanged. 1.1975: Broken up.

LOCHMOR　　　　　　　　　　　　　　　　　　　　　　　　　　*F. W. Hawks*

H3. LOCHMOR (1930-1964)
ON. 161923. 542g. 206n. 155.7 x 29.1 x 9.0
2SCSA 12 cyl: $12\frac{1}{2}''$ — 15'' by L. Gardner and Son Ltd. Manchester. 600bhp. 2 screws. $9\frac{1}{2}$k.

1930: Completed by Ardrossan Dockyard Company Ltd., Ardrossan for David MacBrayne (1928) Ltd. and named LOCHMOR. 1948-49: Re-engined with 12 cyl. Paxman-Ricardo diesels speed now 11 knots. 30.6.1962: Slightly damaged when running aground at Kilmorg Point, Rhum, but refloated. 8.1964: Sold to Tamis S.A. (Panama) renamed AMIMONI and sailed for Greece. Still in Lloyds Register.

H4. LOCHFYNE (1931-1970)
ON. 161949. 656g. 251n. 209.9 x 30.1 x 7.9
4SCSA 10 cyl: $15\frac{3}{4}''$ — 20'' by Davey Paxman & Company Ltd., Colchester coupled to Electric Motors by Metropolitan Vickers Electrical Company Ltd., Manchester. 1400bhp. 2 screws. 16k.
1931: Completed by W. Denny Brothers Ltd., Dumbarton for David MacBrayne (1928) Ltd. and named LOCHFYNE. 1970: Sold to Northern Slipway Ltd. Dublin (British Flag) named unchanged. 1973: Sold to Scottish and Newcastle Breweries Ltd., Edinburgh and renamed OLD LOCHFYNE. 3.1974: Sold to W. H. Arnott Young and Company Ltd. arrived Dalmuir, 25.3.1974: for demolition.

THE ARGENTINE NAVIGATION COMPANY

The Argentine Navigation Company was remarkable in the R.M.S.P. Group in that it was entirely Argentine based, its principal services being an express overnight service between Buenos Aires and Montevideo, and extensive feeder services up the River Plate and other Argentine rivers.

The first combined fleet on these services was La Platense Flotilla, which succeeded a French venture and was for a time under control of Denny Bros. of Dumbarton. This concern failed in December 1890 and an Argentine controlled company was formed, which, by 1906, had come into the ownership of Nicholas Mihanovich, who had owned and operated steamers for many years.

Mihanovich sold out to a consortium of R.M.S.P., Lamport and Holt, Chargeurs Reunis, and Ansaldo in 1917. The R.M.S.P./Lamport and Holt interest was bought in 1931 by Alberto Dodero.

The company was nationalised, without compensation, by the Peron Government in 1949. Following the fall of this regime, the Argentine Merchant Fleet was re-organised in 1962 and 1971, after which the remaining ships were sold to other owners.

MADRID   *Raul Maya Collection Montevideo*

FLEET LIST

D1. MADRID (1925-1936)
1121g. 782n. 1770d. 275.0 x 42.1 x 12.0
4SCSA 12 cyl: $15\frac{3}{4}''$ — $29\frac{1}{2}''$. 1180bhp. 2 screws. 11k.
1925: Completed by A. & J. Inglis Ltd., Glasgow for the Argentine Navigation Company (Nicolas Mihanovich) Ltd., Buenos Aires, and named MADRID. 1931: Owners became Compania Argentina de Navigacion Mihanovich. 25.9.1936: Reported beached following a collision near Ramallo, being completely submerged and believed a total loss, while on passage Buenos Aires — Asuncion. However, continued to appear in Lloyds Register until 1948-9.

ROMA

D2. ROMA (1926-1971)
1121g. 782n. 1770d. 275.0 x 42.1 x 12.0
4SCSA 12 cyl: 15$\frac{3}{4}$" — 29$\frac{1}{2}$". 1180bhp. 11k.
1926: Completed by A. & J. Inglis Ltd., Glasgow for the Argentine Navigation Company (Nicolas
Mihanovich) Ltd., and named ROMA. 1932: Owners became Compania Argentina de Navigacion
Mihanovich. 1941: Owners became Compania Argentina de Navigacion Dodero SA. 1949: Owners
became Compania de Navigacion Fluvial Argentina SA. 1962: Owners became Flota Fluvial del
Estado Argentina. 1971-2: Sold to Abraham Oro y Cia Buenos Aires, name unchanged. Gross
Tonnage now 878, Net Tonnage 472.

D3. IGUAZU (1927-1967)
523g. 294n. 131.8 x 34.0 x 7.7
2SCSA 12 cyl: 13$\frac{1}{4}$" — 15" by L. Gardner and Son Ltd., Manchester. 1200bhp. 2 screws. 11k.
1927: Completed by A. & J. Inglis Ltd., Glasgow for the Argentine Navigation Company (Nicolas
Mihanovich) Ltd., Buenos Aires, and named IGUAZU. 1931: Owners became Compania Argentina
de Navigacion Mihanovich. 1941: Owners became Compania Argentina de Navigacion Dodero
SA. 1949: Owners became Compania de Navigacion Fluvial Argentina SA. 1962: Owners became
Flota Argentina de Navigacion Fluvial. 1967: Broken up.

D4. QUITADOR (1927-1971)
135g. 9n. 100.0 x 21.0 x 9.2
2SCSA 8 cyl: 15" — 16$\frac{1}{2}$" by J. & C. G. Bolinders Company 1240bhp. 2 screws. 14k.
1927. Completed by J. Crichton and Company Ltd., Saltney for the Argentina Navigation Company
(Nicolas Mihanovich) Ltd., and named QUITADOR. 1931: Owners became Compania Argentina
de Navigacion Mihanovich. 1943: Owners became Compania Argentina de Navigacion Dodero
SA. 1949: Owners became Compania de Navigacion Fluvial Argentina SA. 1962: Owners became
Flota Argentina de Navigacion Fluvial. 1966-7: Disappears from Lloyds Register on grounds that
vessel is not sea-going.

D5. AGUARAY (1928-1971)
479g. 333n. 160.0 x 34.0 x 8.6/7.7
8 cyl: by J. & C. G. Bolinders Company Ltd., Skelmersdale. 6600bhp. 2 screws 9½k.
1928: Completed by H. Robb Ltd., Leith for the Argentine Navigation Company (Nicolas
Mihanovich) Ltd., Buenos Aires, and named AGUARAY. 1931: Owners became Compania
Argentina de Navigacion Mihanovich. 1941: Owners became Compania Argentina de Navigacion
Dodero SA. 1949: Owners became Compania de Navigacion Fluvial Argentina SA. 1962: Owners
became Flota Argentina de Navigacion Fluvial. 1971: Owners became Flota Fluvial del Estado
Argentina. 1971-2: Sold to Abraham Oro y Compania Buenos Aires, name unchanged. Still in
service.

BERLIN subsequently **ATENAS**   *Raul Maya Collection Montevideo*

D6. BERLIN (1928-1971)
561g. 301n. 1331d. 228.3 x 36.1 x 10.8/10.5

8 cyl: $9\frac{5}{8}''-12\frac{1}{6}''$ by Soc. Anon. Ansaldo Genoa. 6600bhp. 2 screws. 9½k.

1928: Completed by Carmela Uruguay for the Argentine Navigation Company (Nicolas Mihanovich) Ltd., Buenos Aires, and named BERLIN. 1931: Owners became Compania Argentina de Navigacion Mihanovich. 1941: Renamed ATENAS. Owners became Compania Argentina de Navigacion Dodero SA. 1949: Owners became Compania de Navigacion Fluvial Argentina SA. 1962: Owners became Flota Argentina de Navigacion Fluvial. 1971: Owners became Flota Fluvial del Estado Argentina. 1971-2: Sold to Nicolas Castellani, Buenos Aires, name unchanged. Still in service.

QUITADOR   *Clwyd County Record Office*

D7. AMBERES (1929-1968)
1507g. 859n. 1825d. 275.1 x 43.2 x 12.3/11.2

4SCSA 12 cyl: $15\frac{3}{4}''-29\frac{1}{2}''$. 1180bhp. 2 screws. 11k.

1929: Completed by A. & J. Inglis Ltd., Glasgow for the Argentine Navigation Company (Nicolas Mihanovich) Ltd., and named AMBERES. 1931: Owners became Compania Argentina de Navigacion Mihanovich. 1941: Owners became Compania Argentina de Navigacion Dodero SA. 1949: Owners became Compania de Navigacion Fluvial Argentina SA. 1962: Owners became Flota Argentina de Navigacion Fluvial. 1968-9: Sold to Empresa de Navigacion Samuel Gutaisky, Buenos Aires, name unchanged. 6.1970: Sold for breaking up locally, but still in existence in November 1983.

Raul Maya Collection Montevideo

CIUDAD DE CORRIENTES

AMBERES *Raul Maya Collection Montevideo*

D8. APA (1929-1971)

247g. 152n. 167.4 × 34.0 × 8.2/8.1
Engines by J. & C. Bolinders Company Ltd., Skelmersdale. 3 screws.
1929: Completed by Carmelo Uruguay for the Argentine Navigation Company (Nicolas Mihanovich) Ltd., Buenos Aires and named APA. 1931: Owners became Compania Argentina de Navigacion Mihanovich. 1941: Owners became Compania Argentina de Navigacion Dodero SA. 1949: Owners became Compania de Navigacion Fluvial Argentina SA. 1962: Owners became Flota Argentina de Navigacion Fluvial. 1971: Owners became Flota Fluvial del Estado Argentina. Sold to Arenera 9 de Juilio Buenos Aires, name unchanged. Still in service.

BARCELONA *Raul Maya Collection Montevideo*

D9. BARCELONA (1929-1969)

1507g. 859n. 1825d. 175.0 × 43.1 × 11.7/11.2
4SCSA 12 cyl: $15\frac{3}{4}'' - 29\frac{1}{2}''$. 1180bhp. 2 screws. 11k.
1929: Completed by Harland & Wolff Ltd., Glasgow for the Argentine Navigation Company (Nicolas Mihanovich) Ltd., Buenos Aires, and named BARCELONA. 1931: Owners became Compania Argentina de Navigacion Mihanovich. 1941: Owners became Compania Argentina de Navigacion Fluvial Dodero SA. 1949: Owners became Compania de Navigacion Argentina SA. 1962: Owners became Flota Argentina de Navigacion Fluvial. 1969-70: Sold to Domingo Cacca SA, Buenos Aires, name unchanged. 1973-4: Broken up.

CARDIFF   *Raul Maya Collection Montevideo*

D10. CARDIFF (1929-1969)

1507g. 859n. 1812d. 275.1 x 43.2 x 12.3
4SCSA 12 cyl: $15\frac{3}{4}'' - 29\frac{1}{2}''$. 1180bhp. 2 screws. 11k.

1929: Completed by A. & J. Inglis Ltd., Glasgow for the Argentine Navigation Company (Nicolas Mihanovich) Ltd., and named CARDIFF. 1931: Owners became Compania Argentina de Navigacion Mihanovich. 1941: Owners became Compania Argentina de Navigacion Dodero SA. 1949: Owners became Compania de Navigacion Fluvial Argentina SA. 1962: Owners became Flota Argentina de Navigacion Fluvial. 1969-70: Sold to Domingo Caccia SA, Buenos Aires, name unchanged. Still in service.

CIUDAD DE ASUNCION   *Raul Maya Collection Montevideo*

D11. CIUDAD DE ASUNCION (1929-1963)

2330g. 1453n. 834d. 306.4 x 58.5 x 9.4/7.8
4SCSA 18 cyl: $15\frac{3}{4}'' - 29\frac{1}{2}''$. 1770bhp. 3 screws. 11k.

1929: Completed By A. & J. Inglis Ltd., Glasgow for the Argentine Navigation Company (Nicolas Mihanovich) Ltd., and named CIUDAD DE ASUNCION. 1931: Owners became Compania Argentina de Navigacion Mihanovich. 1941: Owners became Compania Argentina de Navigacion Dodero SA. 1949: Owners became Compania de Navigacion Fluvial Argentina SA. 1962: Owners became Flota Argentina de Navigacion Fluvial. 11.7.1963: While on passage Montevideo to Buenos Aires struck the wreck of Greek "Marionga J. Cairis" in thick fog. The collision holed CIUDAD DE ASUNCION causing a short circuit which resulted in fire breaking out and vessel subsequently sinking.

D12. GLASGOW (1929-1965)

1507g. 859n. 1812d. 275.1 x 43.2 x 12.3/11.2
4SCSA 12 cyl: $15\frac{3}{4}$" — $29\frac{1}{2}$". 1180bhp. 2 screws. 11k.

1929: Completed by A. & J. Inglis Ltd., Glasgow for the Argentine Navigation Company (Nicolas Mihanovich) Ltd., and named GLASGOW. 1931: Owners became Compania Argentina de Navigacion Mihanovich. 1941: Owners became Compania Argentina de Navigacion Dodero SA. 1949: Owners became Compania de Navigacion Fluvial Argentina SA. 1962: Owners became Flota Argentina de Navigacion Fluvial. 1965: Broken up at Buenos Aires.

GLASGOW   *Raul Maya Collection Montevideo*

D13. HAMBURGO (1930-1971)

1507g. 859n. 1825d. 275.1 x 43.2 x 12.3/11.2
4SCSA 12 cyl: $15\frac{3}{4}$" — $29\frac{1}{2}$". 1180bhp. 2 screws. 11k.

1930: Completed by A. & J. Inglis Ltd., Glasgow for the Argentine Navigation Company (Nicolas Mihanovich) Ltd., and named HAMBURGO. 1931: Owners became Compania Argentina de Navigacion Mihanovich. 1941: Renamed BELFAST. Owners became Compania Argentina de Navigacion Dodero SA. 1949: Owners became Compania de Navigacion Fluvial Argentina SA. 1962: Owners became Flota Argentina de Navigacion Fluvial. 1971: Owners became Flota Fluvial del Estado Argentina. 1971-2: Sold to Mariano R. Stabile, Buenos Aires, name unchanged. Still in service.

D14. CIUDAD DE CONCEPCION (1930-1971)

545g. 195n. 200.0 x 37.0 x 8.0/6.2
4SCSA 12 cyl: $12\frac{3}{16}$" — $21\frac{5}{8}$". 800bhp. 2 screws. 12k.

1930: Completed by A. & J. Inglis Ltd., Glasgow for the Argentine Navigation Company (Nicolas Mihanovich) Ltd., and named CIUDAD DE CONCEPCION. 1931: Owners became Compania Argentina de Navigacion Mihanovich. 1941: Owners became Compania Argentina de Navigacion Dodero SA. 1949: Owners became Compania de Navigacion Fluvial Argentina SA. 1962: Owners became Flota Argentina de Navigacion Fluvial. 1971: Owners became Flota Fluvial del Estado Argentina. 1971-2: Sold to Lorenzi Parisi, Buenos Aires, name unchanged. Still in service.

D15. CIUDAD DE CORRIENTES (1930-1969)

2230g, 1263n, 835d. 306.4 x 58.5 x 9.4

4SCSA 18 cyl: $15\frac{3}{4}'' - 29\frac{1}{2}''$. 1770bhp. 3 screws. 11k.

1930: Completed by A. & J. Inglis Ltd., Glasgow for the Argentine Navigation Company (Nicolas Mihanovich) Ltd., and named CIUDAD DE CORRIENTES. 1931: Owners became Compania Argentina de Navigacion Mihanovich. 1941: Owners became Compania de Navigacion Dodero SA. 1949: Owners became Compania de Navigacion Fluvial Argentina SA. 1962: Owners became Flota Argentina de Navigacion Fluvial. 1966: Laid up. 1968: Withdrawn from service and converted to floating restaurant and night-club at Buenos Aires. 12.1.1969: Caught fire, burnt out, and subsequently stripped internally and broken up.

GENOVA

Raul Maya Collection Montevideo

D16. GENOVA (1930-1971)

1507g. 859n. 1825d. 275.0 x 43.1 x 11.7

4SCSA 12 cyl: $15\frac{3}{4}'' - 29\frac{1}{2}''$. 1180bhp. 2 screws. 11k.

1930: Completed by Harland & Wolff Ltd., Glasgow for the Argentine Navigation Company (Nicolas Mihanovich) Ltd., Buenos Aires, and named GENOVA. 1931: Owners became Compania Argentina de Navigacion Mihanovich. 1941: Owners became Compania Argentina de Navigacion Dodero SA. 1949: Owners became Compania de Navigacion Fluvial Argentina SA. 1962: Owners became Flota Argentina de Navigacion Fluvial. 1970: Sold to Osvaldo G. Astarita y Cia Buenos Aires, renamed QUEBRACHO and broken up at Campana, Argentina 3.1972.

D17. GUAYRA (1930-1971)

785g. 448n. 170.0 x 36.0 x 8.0/6.2

4SCSA 12 cyl: $12\frac{3}{16}'' - 21\frac{5}{8}''$. 800bhp. 2 screws. 11k.

1930: Completed by A. & J. Inglis Ltd., Glasgow for the Argentine Navigation Company (Nicolas Mihanovich) Ltd., and named GUAYRA. 1931: Owners became Compania Argentina de Navigacion Mihanovich. 1941: Owners became Compania Argentina de Navigacion Dodero SA. 1949: Owners became Compania de Navigacion Fluvial Argentina SA. 1962: Owners became Flota Argentina de Navigacion Fluvial. 1971: Owners became Flota Fluvial del Estado Argentina. 1971-2: Sold to Lineas Oceanicas Americanas SA, Buenos Aires, name unchanged. Still in service.

OPERATING EXPERIENCE

One of the more remarkable facts to emerge from the study of the introduction and development of the motorship in the fleets of the Kylsant Group is the apparently haphazard manner in which the diesel engine was introduced to the various fleets.

The first company to operate motorships was Glen Line, who owned 6 by 1919, a seventh, actually the first built, having been lost during the war. Despite this, at least two other companies, Moss Hutchinson and Lamport and Holt built steamers similar in design to their new motorships for comparative trials. In another case, Union-Castle, the first motorship ordered was originally planned as a steamship although the parent R.M.S.P. had already ordered its two large diesel engined liners. It was an initiative from Harland & Wolff which led to CARNARVON CASTLE emerging in 1926 with diesels, admittedly at additional cost of some £50,000 and with an assurance that the builders would carry any further costs themselves. There are also no signs of any significant interchange of operational experience between the companies, notably between Union-Castle and R.M.S.P. who from 1925-1930 were the only two lines using large, and comparable, diesel engined liners on express routes.

The first batch of motorships, the early Glen Liners, did not serve their original owners for very long. 5 were transferred to other lines, one almost immediately going to Elder Dempsters for conversion to a passenger liner and the other 4 to P.S.N.C. in 1923 for the South American service. It is highly likely that this was occasioned by operational requirements as they were replaced by 5 considerably larger and slightly faster vessels between 1922 and 1924, and therefore too much importance should not be attached to this.

The obvious question which requires an answer is simply "Did they work?" It has to be recognised that in replying "Yes" the reply refers as much to the engineers as to the engines. A glance down the fleet lists, and consideration of the length of service of many of the ships indicates that owners' requirements were met, but at a price. John Lamb recalled his experiences as Second Engineer aboard one of the early diesel engined tankers, twin screw and owned by Eagle Tankers. He noted that frequently one engine at least was out of action, and during a three month voyage only 5 out of 64 crankshaft, crankpin and crosshead bearings had not been remetalled. Every piston had been removed, some several times, to free piston rings and 7 had been renewed because heads had fractured, while 5 cylinder covers had cracked and needed replacing. Overheating proved a major headache, combated by 100 gallons of lubricating oil daily, laboriously emptied from barrels on deck and carried below by bucket. Engineers did their rounds clad in oil-skins and sou'westers to shield them from the pleasure of an oil bath. It is fair to add that this particular ship was an unfortunate example and was in fact re-engined shortly after John Lamb left her, but it does give an impression of the difficulties which to a greater or lesser extent afflicted the pioneers. Lamb did, though, mention two good points, low fuel consumption and a comparatively cool engine room.

The mention of twin screws draws attention to the fact that most of the early motor-ships were twin screw. Not until 1925 did the Kylsant Group put its trust in a single screw motorship.

Another observer, in the 1920's and 1930's was George Young, for many years Shipping Editor of the Cape Times. A most knowledgeable and dedicated shipping journalist, one of his targets was the apparent attitude of shipowners that whatever they were doing at the time was perfect, even when it wasn't. Little escaped his eagle eye, and he recalled the difficulties inflicted upon engineers by the new engines and not infrequent times when early B. & W. powered motorships laid up for weeks in Cape Town awaiting replacement crankshafts, pistons etc. Generators provided another problem, more especially when the demands of cargo refrigeration were added to those for heat and light. This problem was longer in solving. As late as 1954 the then 4 year old BLOEMFONTEIN CASTLE had to have her generators replaced after a number of embarrassing breakdowns. Yet all was not bad, CARNARVON CASTLE was almost unique in retaining her 1926 generators throughout her 36 years service.

Many of the difficulties stemmed from the fact that most of the motorships were operated on liner routes with at least some degree of scheduling, so that there was some element of running against the clock. The Glen Line ships required constant maintenance even though their schedule was relatively easy, and in fact some were to serve over 30 years. There was one group of ships which proved virtually trouble-free from the start. These were the Dodd, Thomson tramps.

The Dodd, Thomson tramps, the "Kings", were all powered by the reliable 6 cylinder

$29\frac{1}{8}''$ — $59\frac{1}{16}''$ engine, of which 20 were built for Group ships, as well as 12 examples of an 8 cylinder version. The 6 cylinder engine was capable of developing 3,100bhp and in this form powered DUNBAR CASTLE, her two engines driving her 10,000 tons gross at 13.5 knots, using 20 tons of oil daily. Examples fitted on the "Kings" and other cargo vessels were derated to 1,850bhp giving trial speeds of 12.5 knots and an ability to carry 7,500 tons of cargo and 800 tons fuel oil at 10 knots using 8 tons of oil daily at most. Captain George Smith, O.B.E., commanded KING JOHN throughout the 1930's and a sistership after the war and confirmed that none of these 11 ships suffered any engine trouble other than routine annual maintenance. This points to an interesting fact, namely that accidentally rather than by intention Dodd, Thomson had discovered that the diesel engine operated more satisfactorily if it was not being pressed to maximum performance for prolonged periods. Appreciation of this would have come too late to be of help to the Group, if it had been realised, since the collapse was well under way when the "Kings" entered service. The point was not appreciated, though, as indicated in the chapter on the express liners, possibly because Sir Vernon Thomson, who was in a position to find out, understood profits and balance sheets and shipping but did not understand ships. Put another way, he realised that the diesel engine had carried his company through a crisis, was economical on fuel, and also reliable, but he did not know why. As a result Union-Castle persisted with diesel engines and found themselves facing more problems in the postwar years with war weary ships pressed to maintain schedules only just within their capabilities when new.

The period of transition from steam to diesel was not a rapid or particularly glamorous part of maritime history, after all, except in 'The Mikado' there is nothing glamorous in being boiled in oil. In many cases it was exasperating and messy. Where it is claimed that "the ships proved satisfactory in service" it must be remembered that this too often meant that the owners' requirements were met because engine room staff worked like trojans in difficult conditions keeping the propellers turning at the necessary speed. Yet the inherent ability of the diesels to do what was needed was proven, if only by the least exalted of the owners in the Group. The years passed, techniques improved, and engines became more powerful. The Glen Line motorships of the late 1930's and their opposite numbers in Union-Castle showed what could be done on a grander scale, and today has seen the steam engine largely eclipsed. None of this would have been achieved so quickly had it not been for those early engineers in their oilskins replacing parts time and time again, nor would it have been achieved without Lord Pirrie's foresight in taking the opportunity to build the engines and Lord Kylsant's courage in buying them. Two of those engines are still in service today, 54 years old, in Chinese waters powering m.v. GUANG HUA ex HIGHLAND PRINCESS.

LOCHFYNE   *F. W. Hawks*

THE EXPRESS LINERS

Most of the ships in this volume were either cargo or cargo-passenger, but there were large and fast passenger liners of which 5 merit special consideration. They were not the largest nor yet the fastest ships, but they were built to maintain their owners' express Royal Mail services run to demanding schedules which proved a stringent test of their mechanical capability and reliability.

The term 'express' may need explanation. 16 knots scarcely conveys an image of the ocean greyhound, but in the 1920's it was a fair speed for any regular ocean service other than the North Atlantic and the Trans-Pacific routes. During the 1920's only Orient Line, with their magnificent fleet of 5 18 knot 20,000 ton liners, and a few P & O liners of 17 knots exceeded it. Like so many other terms 'express' is relative, and even today South African citizens would look askance if the pride of their Railway system, the luxurious Blue Train, were not described as 'express', although its average 40 m.p.h. is well below that of other trains in other countries.

The five liners were:

Name	Length B.P.	Beam	G.R.T.	Operating Speed
ALCANTARA)	630'	78'	22,000	16 knots
ASTURIAS)				
CARNARVON CASTLE	630'	73'	20,000	15½ knots
WINCHESTER CASTLE	630'	75'	20,000	15½ knots
WARWICK CASTLE	650'	75'	20,400	15½ knots

It will be observed that all five were of similar dimensions, size, and speed. The two Royal Mail liners were of completely new design for that company, while CARNARVON CASTLE was initially ordered as a follow-up to two four-funnelled steamers and was of identical length and one foot additional beam. The two W class ships enjoyed a small increase in beam, and WARWICK CASTLE for some reason which avaailable records do not make clear was given an additional 20' length. The first three had identical engines, those on the last two were of slightly greater bore, being 8 cylinder versions of the 10 cylinder engines fitted aboard BRITANNIC and GEORGIC. The increase in power was not material, and maximum power available in theory was 13,000bhp to 14,000bhp.

By 1933 both Royal Mail Lines and Union-Castle had come under considerable commercial and political pressure to improve their services. The dilemma facing the South American company was the first to be resolved as, in the face of competition from Germany's 21 knot CAP ARCONA and France's new L'ATLANTIQUE. The decision was taken to re-engine the two A class ships to increase their speed to about 18 knots and, when funds permitted, to build a third ship. At the same time Union-Castle were seriously embarrassed by the decision of the South African Government to subsidise a Lloyd Triestino service between Genoa and South African ports. The two ships were marginally larger than Union-Castle's WARWICK CASTLE but some 4 knots faster. The regular sight of the mailship being overtaken by these interlopers boded no good. Accordingly Union-Castle, under their new regime, set about the challenge.

The solutions found by the companies were diametrically opposed. Royal Mail abandoned the diesel and installed steam turbines in the A ships as well as in the 1939 built ANDES. Union-Castle built 3 new and much larger and faster mailships and re-engined a further 5. Also added were 4 intermediate passenger ships, 6 refrigerated cargo liners, and one small coaster. Of this programme, only 2 of the re-engined mailships employed steam turbines, all the rest were diesel powered.

The stated reason for Royal Mail's decision to revert to steam turbines was that the latter would provide a smoother running engine and also that the diesel was not entirely suitable for high speed liner service. There had been adverse comment on the level of vibration aboard these two ships and also on the Castles, as well as claims of excessive noise in the engine rooms. It would appear, though, that the two points were linked.

The relevant factor is that although all five ships were similarly powered the two largest and beamiest were required to operate half a knot faster than the other three. In this connection the trial speeds of two of the ships are relevant, although such figures should be regarded with utmost caution and too much should not be read into them. Briefly, CARNARVON CASTLE made 18.4 knots on the measured mile while WINCHESTER CASTLE made only 17.36 knots. The difference, after considering possible variations in weather and other pertinent variables is hardly worth mentioning,

ALCANTARA after re-engining   *A. S. Mallett Collection*

CARNARVON CASTLE after re-engining   *A. Duncan*

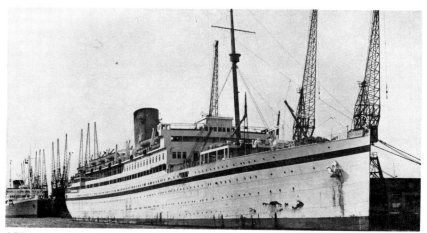

ASTURIAS postwar as an emigrant ship. Astern of her is **WINCHESTER CASTLE** with only one funnel.   *World Ship Photo Library*

but the weight of evidence is that the narrower ship was slightly faster. It would be most surprising if the two Royal Mail ships were any speedier than WINCHESTER CASTLE. The effect of this is that while the Castles had a potential reserve of up to 1½ knots between service and maximum sea-going speed the reserve at the disposal of the A class ships was something under 1 knot. Given these circumstances the Royal Mail decision was almost inevitable.

Union Castle meanwhile persisted with the diesel, which had kept the new Deputy Chairman's King Line going, and the engines had given no trouble at all. James Gray. the Superintendent Engineer, was also in favour and he ought to know as he had worked for Harland & Wolff, who were producing a new engine that would suffice to drive a 25,000 ton liner at 19 knots with 20% power in reserve. Accordingly two such ships were ordered and a third slightly larger ship followed. When STIRLING CASTLE, ran her trials the unfortunate discovery was made that there were doubts as to whether her engines could develop the necessary reserve power. In practice it emerged that the new ships could maintain up to 19½ knots for prolonged periods, perhaps a little more in the case of the two smaller ships. CARNARVON CASTLE, WINCHESTER CASTLE and WARWICK CASTLE were re-engined with engines of similar power and proved capable of 20–20½ knots sea speed. The new schedule came into operation on 22 December 1938 and the required speed of the mailships was now 18.6 knots.

There was little problem with vibration on any of these Castles, until late in the career of CARNARVON CASTLE, when she was running at maximum capacity continually, the reserve of power sufficing to eliminate this fault. Nevertheless after the Second World War maintaining the schedule became ever more difficult and the fact that this was done was as much a tribute to the dedication of the engine room staff as it was to the diesel technology. The ugly problem of skin friction now reared its head to join those already engendered by the strains of wartime operation and comparative neglect of maintenance. The table below illustrates the effect over the years upon one ship CARNARVON CASTLE.

Year	Max. Revs.	Equivalent speed	Notes
1938	120	21 knots	Design specification
1938	116	20 knots	Record voyage September described as 'not quite all out'
1953	112	19.3 knots	
1962	108	18.9 knots	Effectively the bare minimum to maintain the schedule.

To some extent the other four diesel mailships which survived the war were similarly affected. Yet all five maintained the service for between 23 and 30 years without any serious disruption due to mechanical trouble and indeed the occasions on which the mailship was materially late were so few as to merit immediate press comment. Much was attributable to the ingenuity and devotion of the engineers, but also to the fundamentally robust engines which withstood so many years hard running, the last ten at a continuous 95% or more of full power.

Two smaller liners built for Union-Castle underlined this point, albeit unintentionally. DURBAN CASTLE and PRETORIA CASTLE were completed in 1938 and 1939 to run the 16 knot intermediate service, but with sufficient reserve of speed to stand in on the Mail service, which they did between 1947 and 1950 running at 18 knots. Like the King Line tramps they suffered no mechanical problems. In 1963 Union-Castle again built diesel powered mailships. By now the diesel was capable of producing power far in excess of that likely to be demanded on the Cape service, but no chances were taken, and the two ships, running on a schedule demanding 22½ knots, proved capable of exceeding 25 knots on 60% of power.

Of the other large cargo liners built for Group companies, one, the P.S.N.C. REINA DEL PACIFICO, was to enjoy a long and commercially successful career on the route to Chile, while BRITANNIC and GEORGIC both set new standards on the North Atlantic. None of these was subject to the same strains imposed by their schedules. One final ship should be mentioned, although strictly not part of this story, Shaw Savill's DOMINION MONARCH. Like REINA DEL PACIFICO she was quadruple screw, and like the Union-Castle liners of similar size war-time stresses ensured that after 1948 she was hard put to maintain her intended speed of 19 knots, and her life of only 23 years was rather shorter than might have been expected for a popular ship, although this was largely attributable to the marketing decision to operate passenger-only ships.

A splendid view of the motorship funnels. WINCHESTER CASTLE on trials.
Union Castle Line

THE FUNNELS

Fifty years after the last of the Pirrie-Kylsant motorships entered service the best remembered feature is the famous 'Harland & Wolff' twin funnels, the foremost set close abaft the bridge and both circular in shape and short in stature.

It is not difficult to understand why, since throughout the age of steam the funnel has been the means of displaying a ship's or her owner's individuality, and to this day there are few features which attract more speedy or vehement comment than a funnel which is not deemed appropriate to the ship carrying it.

Amid the welter of views on a funnel's appearance its function is easily forgotten. Early steamships sported a tall thin smokestack, in order to lift the smuts as far from the ship as possible, and also to improve draught to the boilers. The fact that many were originally painted black was as much due to their function and its practical effects as to choice, and when early owners such as Cunard or Alfred Holt opted for brighter colours funnel tops remained black. With the invention of the diesel the opportunity was taken to abolish the funnel and this course was followed over many years by the Danish East Asiatic Line, starting with SELANDIA in 1912. Similarly the first Glen Line cargo motorships of the First World War either made to with an inconspicuous exhaust pipe or with a flowerpot funnel which was easily concealed, as the photograph below shows. Evidently this was not to the liking of other Group owners or indeed of Glen Line, for the succeeding series of motorships, built between 1920 and 1925, reverted to the style of funnel adopted by contemporary steam powered vessels. Then, in 1925, ASTURIAS emerged from Belfast with her twin funnels, and a tradition was born. It cannot be claimed that the new design constituted classic beauty but equally there was an impression of bulk and power to be found in the solid, squat profile presented. Eventually there were 11 ocean going liners of this design plus a further 6 built to a slightly modified design for Nelson Line. On a smaller scale the four Irish Sea ferries, two of the River Plate ferries and MacBraynes LOCHFYNE were built to a similar profile.

The new style funnels were not restricted to the passenger ships. Those on the King Line and Elder Dempster cargo ships of the later 1920's and 1930 reflected the new style, and two slightly earlier Elder Dempster liners, ACCRA and APAPA, boasted single funnels only of the ASTURIAS type, dispensing with the fore funnel, which in every case was a dummy. It must be said, though, that some considered the result visually detrimental, and the owners' decision to fit two funnels aboard ACHIMOTA may have been influenced by this viewpoint.

LAUTARO. The funnel is completely obscured by the lighthouse behind the ship.
Furness Withy Group P.R. Dept.

CONCLUSION

When the last of the Pirrie-Kylsant motorships entered service in 1932 the dismantling of the Group itself was well under way. In the period of 17 years since the first diesel ship joined Glen Line immense strides had been made, and the motorship was firmly established on the seven seas. This was an achievement of which Lords Pirrie and Kylsant could well be proud, had the first lived long enough to see it and the second been in a position to further exploit it. In addition to the Group's own motorships large numbers were engined and built by Harland & Wolff for other owners, notably the Bank Line.

From the early, and often temperamental engines of low power larger and more reliable machines had been developed, culminating in the outstandingly reliable 6 cylinder engines which powered so many of the later cargo ships, and the large engines fitted aboard the two White Star liners. Undoubtedly there would have been further ships of this class but for economic reasons, as there would have been at least one additional Union-Castle intermediate and possibly a sister for REINA DEL PACIFICO. More problematic is the OCEANIC, recently the subject of attention. Details released indicate that she would have been a three funnelled version of BRITANNIC with 47 diesel engines driving electric motors and totalling some 200,000bhp. Whether this fascinating exercise in technology would in practice have proved practicable is beyond the scope of this work, but experience with the larger and faster passenger motorships up to World War Two is not encouraging in this respect, and the impression remains that OCEANIC might well have proved another example of trying to run before one could walk. This does not diminish the achievements of the motorships and the men who created and operated them. The vision of the designers, builders and owners, and the skill and dedication of the engineers who, often by dint of long hours of sweaty toil in trying conditions kept the early motorships moving albeit on reduced power while one part after another was removed, repaired or substituted, and then replaced, is now bearing fruit in the majority of the world's sea lanes. Even as this book goes to press the Cunard Line, successors to White Star, have revealed that they are investigating the possibility of re-engining QUEEN ELIZABETH 2 with diesels. The debt owed to Lord Pirrie and Lord Kylsant for their determination to build technologically advanced ships half a century ago is considerable, and should not be forgotten.

HIGHLAND PRINCESS now GUANG HUA　　　　　*World Ship Photo Library*

ACKNOWLEDGEMENTS

The authors wish to express their gratitude to the undermentioned persons and companies for the welcome assistance and co-operation they have received while preparing this book.

The advice and facilities of the World Ship Society and in particular members responsible for the Central Record and Photograph Library were invaluable, as was also advice from Michael Crowdy in the preparation and planning of this book. Further information relating to the ships was obtained from back numbers of Marine News and Sea Breezes, and Ships Monthly, also from histories of certain of the owning companies, most of which are now out of print, and from the Public Relations Departments of Ocean Transport and Trading plc, Furness Withy plc and British and Commonwealth Shipping Co. plc. Valuable historical background has been found in 'A Business of National Importance' by Edwin Green and Michael Moss (Methuen, 1982) and this book is strongly commended to any reader seeking a deeper understanding of the history of the Kylsant Group.

The authors are indebted to the World Ship Society for permission to reproduce material from 'Idyll of the Kings' by Alan Mallett, to Heinemann's for permission to reproduce an extract from Lord Sanderson of Ayot's memoirs 'Of Ships and Sealing Wax', and to Michael Bustard for permission to use material from his father Frank Bustard's unpublished memoirs.

Harland & Wolff Ltd. have patiently answered all the authors' questions and provided photographs from their archives. Thanks are due to other providers of illustrations, all acknowledged in situ. To Raul Maya, of Montevideo, thanks are additionally due for up-dated information on the Argentine Navigation Co. motorships. Assistance in copying photographs has been given by Michael Speedy and David Grieve, both of Wroxham, while Sally Leyshon, Anne Tims, and Rosemary Gladstone have converted the authors' manuscript into typing. Finally, thanks are due to our printers for their help and advice, and to Rachel Mockridge and Paul Buckerfield for assisting in proof reading.

February 1984

DEIDO with taller funnel   *World Ship Photo Library*

INDEX OF SHIPS' NAMES

Glenogle	G10	14 50	46
Glenshiel	G14	14 51	51
Glentara	G9	13 50	
	E11	34	34
Guayra	D17	16 108	
Hamburgo	D13	15 107	
Henry Stanley	E14	15 36	36
Highland Brigade	N3	17 69	19 68 69
Highland Chieftain	N2	17 68	68
Highland Hope	N4	17 69	
Highland Monarch	N1	17 67	67
Highland Patriot	N6	17 69	66
Highland Princess	N5	17 69 110	116
Iguazu	D3	102	
Innisfallen	I4	16 99	96
Karamea	S4	19 94	92
Kheti	MH1	19 71	70
King Arthur	K9	15 84	10
King Edgar	K3	15 82	80
King Edwin	K4	15 82	
King Egbert	K5	15 83	83
King James	K1	15 79 82	82
King John	K6	15 83	83
King Lud	K7	15 84	84
King Malcolm	K2	15 79 82	81
King Neptune	K8	15 84	85 Endpaper
King Stephen	K10	15 84	85
King William	K11	15 85	84
Kufra	MH2	19 71	71
Kwaibo	E12	35	35
Lagarto	P5	44	44
	G4	13 48	
Laguna	P4	14 43	43
La Paz	P1	13 41	42
Lassell	L3	14 54	52
Lautaro	P6	44	115
	G2	13 47 48	
Leighton	L1	13 54	53
Linnell	L2	14 54	54
Llangibby Castle	UC2	15 63	63
Lobos	P2	13 43	42
Lochearn	H2	100	7
Lochfyne	H4	100 115	110
Lochgoil	R1	14 20	7
Lochkatrine	R2	14 20	23 59
Lochmonar	R3	14 24	23 24
Lochmor	H3	100	100
Lochshiel	H1	100	
Loreto	P7	44	44
	G6	13 49	49
Loriga	P8	44	11
	G7	14 49	
Losada	P3	13 43	43
Macgregor Laird	E19	15 38	38
Madrid	D1	15 101	101
Mary Kingsley	E16	19 36	36
Mary Slessor	E17	15 37	37

Mattawin	E3	13 29	30
Milverton	E11	13 34	34
	G9	13 50	
Pacheco	A4	15 75	75
Palacio	A3	15 74	74
Pelayo	A5	15 75	
Pinto	A6	15 75	72
Pinzon	A1	19 73	73
Pizarro	A2	19 74	74
Ponzano	A7	15 75	103
Quitador	D4	102	10
Reina Del Pacifico	P9	16 41 45 113 115	16 40 45
Roma	D2	15 102	102
Taranaki	S2	19 93	93
Ulster Monarch	I1	16 97 98	98
Ulster Prince	I3	16 99	12
Ulster Queen	I2	16 98	99
Warwick Castle	UC5	17 65 111 113	61 65
William Wilberforce	E18	15 38	37
Winchester Castle	UC4	17 64 111 113	56 65 114
Zealandic	S1	19 91	93 94

FINISHED WITH ENGINES

DARDANAS formerly GLENAPP (II) being broken up at Inverkeithing in August 1957. Astern of her are the FRANCONIA and CITY OF CANBERRA *A. S. Mallett*

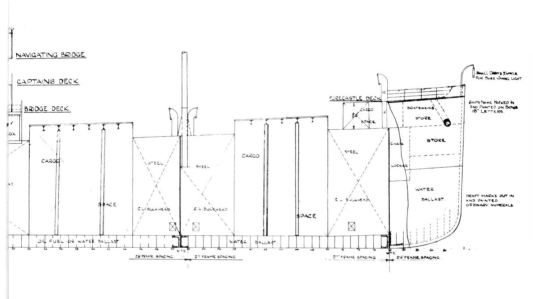

NAVIGATING BRIDGE

CAPTAINS DECK

BRIDGE DECK.

FORECASTLE DECK

SMALL DAVIT & TACKLE
FOR SUEZ CANAL LIGHT

SHIPS NAME NICKED IN
AND PAINTED ON BOWS
18" LETTERS.

BOATSWAINS
STORE

CARGO
SPACE

CARGO

CARGO

STEEL

STORE

STEEL

STEEL

CHAIN

CARGO

C.L.BULKHEAD

C.L.BULKHEAD

LOCKER

C.L.BULKHEAD

WATER
BALLAST

DRAFT MARKS CUT IN
AND PAINTED
ORDINARY NUMERALS.

SPACE

SPACE

OIL FUEL OR WATER BALLAST

WATER BALLAST

28 FRAME SPACING

27 FRAME SPACING

27 FRAME SPACING

24 FRAME SPACING

A. S. Mallett Collection